Supervision in Youth Work

by M Joan Tash

The report of a two-year training project in which selected youth
workers acquired skill in supervising

University of
Chester
Warrington Campus

University of Chester Library
Tel: 01925 534284

*Published for the YMCA George Williams College and M J Tash by the
YMCA George Williams College, 199 Freemasons Road, Canning Town,
London E16 3PY*

NCSS reference number 740
NCSS printed 1967
NCSS reprinted 1969
YMCA reprinted 1984
YMCA reprinted 2000

Printed by The Good News Press Ltd., Essex

I am delighted that with the agreement of the N.C.V.O. (N.C.S.S.), who published this book seventeen years ago, it is now to be reprinted.

It is particularly appropriate that it should be republished by the YMCA National College. From its beginning, the College has encouraged and supported supervision and the training of supervisors. I was responsible for this training for ten years, and Margaret Murray has continued similar training for the last four years. Field-work supervision is seen to be as essential as tutoring in the training of students.

In seventeen years, understanding of supervision in youth work has been deepened and extended. I was tempted to add to this book; but it was a description and analysis of a project, so although I realise that more could have been extracted at the time, I think it must now remain untouched. Hopefully, as its content is basic, it has withstood the test of time. Certainly the examples are repeated many times today.

The issues around supervision are also similar. For those debating management and supervision pages 158 and 159 indicate that this is not new – apart from the use of the word 'management'. This book could never be called 'non-managerial' supervision. It describes positive work developed to meet the needs of workers. This has a life of its own – not to be considered negatively in relation to other work.

Articles have been written about supervision in the Youth Service. It is sad that so little is being written to provide material based on sound evidence, when there are those who must have such material. I hope the writing will not be left to those, perhaps with less training and experience, who prefer to dwell on titles – personal, developmental, managerial, non-managerial, rent-a-friend – and then try to fit parts of supervision into their patterns. This simply causes confusion in the profession particularly to the newly qualified. The question will always remain – should training (including supervision) be geared to the needs of organisers, managers, academics or assessors, or to the needs of workers, students and volunteers? The former is usually tidier, but the latter of more value.

If a republished book could be dedicated, it would be to the many supervisors I know, and those I do not know, who have committed themselves for many years to training and practice, because they recognised the value of supervision to new and Inexperienced workers, and students who would soon become workers. Frequently this has been without the understanding, approval or encouragement of administration. Rarely has it been acknowledged financially. The supervisors' satisfaction has been in the development and confidence of those being supervised and in their own developing skills.

Good wishes to you,

M. JOAN TASH

I

WORKERS/SUPERVISORS

Zoe Baker

John High

Malcolm Blakeney

Patrick McCarthy

Derek Cox

Audrey Noble

Bnian Draper

David Sharp

David Dryer

Sylvia Taylor

These workers are described in the report by letters of the alphabet A to K, except in Chapter 10 when all are known as Y

NEW LEADERS/VOLUNTEER SUPERVISEES

Lance Armstrong

Ronald Hockings *(short period)*

Douglas Barrett

Daniel Holland

William Dower

Joseph Lowney

Gillian Dent

Jeremy De Mierre

Cyril Eden

Jill Patrick

Rodney Gilbert

The new leaders are described as X in the report

PROJECT SUPERVISOR

M. Joan Tash

Described in illustrations as S

CONSULTANTS

Josephine Klein *Reader in Social Relations in the University of Sussex*

Joan E. Matthews *Principal Lecturer, National Collegefor the Training of Youth Leaders*

Ilse J. Westheimer *Head Psychiatric Social Worker, Child Guidance Training Centre*

George W. Goetschius *Youth Work Consultant, Young Women's Christian Association*

ADVISORY GROUP

This group consisted of representatives from the following bodies

North and South London Branches of the Compass Society

Youth Service Association

National Association of Youth Officers

National Institute for Social Work Training

Standing Conference of Voluntary Youth Organisations
– Greater London

Standing Conference of Voluntary Youth Organi'sations
– Inner London Committee

London Training Group inner London Education Authority

Department of Education and Science *(Assessor)*

ADMINISTRATION

Kathleen Proud   *General Secretary, London Council of Social Service*
Muriel Smith   *Community Developtnent Officer, London Council of Social Service*

The Community Development Committee *on behalf of* The Executive Committee of the London Council of Social Service

Secretary   Dorothy Lea

FINANCED BY
The Department of Education and Science with a contribution towards the London participants from The Inner London Education Authority

CONTENTS

ACKNOWLEDGMENTS

We should like to acknowledge with sincere thanks the contributions of a number of people to the project described in this report.

Appropriately the first group to be acknowledged consists of the ten selected youth workers, who not only committed themselves to training for two years, but also in addition to their full-time jobs, put in a great deal of extra work in order to help the new leaders whom they supervised. It is true that these workers developed their skills and acquired new ones, but there were moments when they might well have opted out of the extra work and responsibility, which lasted for such a long period, and still continues. Perhaps even more important than the time involved, was the readiness of these workers to allow this report to be written about them, their learning, and their work. They also studied the report as it was being written, made suggestions, and checked its validity. It was due to this group that the nature of supervision in youth work could be described in specific terms, from a practical experience.

Our thanks go also to the new leaders who volunteered to be supervised. They were aware of the experimental nature of this project, and were not deterred by it. The material which they provided, and their evaluation, contributed substantially to the understanding of supervision within the project.

The four consultants by the nature of their contribution were invaluable to the project. In line with the whole approach to the work, they made themselves available individually to the supervisor for consultations about specific problems. They also met several times with the administrators and supervisor, and on occasions with the workers, to discuss different aspects of supervision or youth work. We are indebted to the consultants, not only for their time, but for the way in which they were prepared to share their knowledge and skill.

We express our thanks to the voluntary and statutory bodies who showed their interest through their representatives on the advisory group. The advisory group had the task of hearing reports, making comments and suggestions, and keeping organisations and bodies informed. We are grateful for the way in which they used limited information to develop useful discussions on different aspects of supervision, and its function in the youth service.

We acknowledge with sincere thanks the support of the Department of Education and Science which financed this project, and of the Inner London Education Authority which contributed to the London participants. Their interest was also personified through Miss Newton Smith, H.M.I. (assessor) and Mr R. W. Keeble, Principal Youth Officer, who served on the advisory group.

We should also like to thank all those who, in a short space of time, gave most useful comments on the final draft of the report – consultants, colleagues in the youth service, and members of the London Council of Social Service community development committee – and in particular, Josephine Klein, who read and commented on each chapter as it was written, and Dorothy Lea (secretary) who commented on it as she typed it. Reading and thinking about reports is time-consuming, and we are most grateful for the help given.

The project took place in a room at the Christchurch United Youth Clubs, and we are most grateful to Peter Oliver (Warden) and his wife Joan, for their hospitality and co-operation.

That the project came into being was due entirely to the initiative and perseverance of the North and South London Branches of the Compass Society. This society was formed in January 1962 by some of the first students to complete the course at the National College for the Training of Youth Leaders. Membership is open to anyone who successfully completes the National College course. The purpose of the society is 'to assist members to gain further knowledge of all matters concerning young people, by providing means for the exchange of information, ideas and experience'. The provision of further training opportunities has always been a primary concern of the Society, and the North and South London branches, recognising a need for supervision, studied the possibilities and consulted numerous people in order to launch this project. We are indebted to them for this vital part which they played.

M. JOAN TASH
KATHLEEN PROUD

CHAPTER ONE

The Project in Outline

THE INITIAL STAGES

THE In-service Training Project was conceived by the North and South London branches of the Compass Society. The idea of a project arose from a recognition from their own experience that youth leaders needed to continue their training in their first posts. Supervision as a form of individual training was seen by the society as an appropriate way of meeting this need. At that time supervision as a form of training was a rare possibility for new leaders, and there were few people in the field of youth work who felt equipped to supervise. The Compass Society therefore devised a project which would not only provide supervision on current work, but would be the means of training more experienced youth leaders to supervise new leaders.

When plans were made, the Compass Society invited the London Council of Social Service to sponsor the project. The Council agreed, and the project became attached to its Department for Community Development. The Department of Education and Science agreed to finance the work, and the Inner London Education Authority agreed to make a contribution towards participants from London.

The London Council of Social Service appointed a tutor/supervisor and invited four people to be available to the supervisor for consultations, and also to meet with the administrators and supervisor at intervals in order to discuss the work. The Council also set up an advisory group, consisting of representatives from interested statutory and voluntary bodies. The purpose of this group was to hear reports on the project, to discuss the work, to make suggestions, and to keep their organisations informed.

The purpose of the project was:
(a) To train twelve leaders in techniques of supervision in youth work
(b) To make a report of the project available to establishments training full-time or part-time youth leaders
(c) To provide material on the nature of supervision which would help other youth workers to attempt similar in-service training.

I

The project was to be from September 1964 to December 1966. From September to December 1964 leaders were to be selected. From December 1964 to August 1966 the training was to continue, and from September to December 1966 a report was to be written.

SELECTION OF LEADERS

Letters were sent to all full-time leaders in Greater London, who were qualified and had at least two years' experience in the field, inviting them to apply for participation in the project. Thirty applied, and apart from a few who withdrew on learning more details, all the applicants were interviewed. Normally, the supervisor spent two hours interviewing each leader and, if she felt unable to make a decision about a leader's suitability, he was then interviewed by a consultant. Several leaders withdrew following their interview, when they realised that the training would not be what they had expected, or when they accepted that their strengths were in organisation and administration and not in teaching. Some leaders were not accepted as it was believed that they needed more experience before training others, or that whereas they appeared to have a natural flair for working with young people, they did not seem to have an analytical mind essential to training.

The interviews varied according to the interest of the leader, but all applicants were encouraged to talk about their own work, in detail, to explain what they understood by 'social group work' and 'supervision', to describe their expectations of the project, and to ask questions about it. While this was happening the supervisor was attempting to assess the applicant's attitudes to his work, his understanding of it, and his ability to describe it. She was also concerned with his ability to learn, his flexibility, and his relationships witho adults and young people. Although she had anticipated that knowledge of social group work would be an important factor in selection, it became clear that no two applicants had the same ideas about it, so this was replaced by the capacity to observe and describe what was happening between people. The supervisor also looked for evidence of warmth and feeling towards people, together with an ability to describe the work with detachment. The applicants found the interview not unlike the supervision sessions to follow. They were constantly being asked to explain what they meant, or consider their statements from a different angle. The supervisor was concerned less with what was said than with how it was said, and with the underlying attitudes, skills and feelings which became evident. Her questions and comments were directed towards understanding these.

There was no previous experience which could be used for the selection of potential supervisors, and there was very little common ground from which to make an assessment. The selection was therefore made on the ability and assessed potentiality of an individual for learning and training, taking into account the factors mentioned. Leaders were selected subject to a supporting letter from their youth officers and/or their training officers and subject to the approval of their management committees.

Seven men and three women were selected. One was thirty-eight years and the others were between twenty-five and thirty years. Eight had been trained in the National College for the Training of Youth Leaders, one in Westbill College of Education, one at Morley College. The youth work which they represented included three youth centres administered by different local education authorities; two settlements, one sponsored by a Roman Catholic association, and another by a college; two youth clubs sponsored by a college and a school; a community club affiliated to the Association of Jewish Youth; a new open club sponsored by an Anglican church; and detached work sponsored by a social council. In all cases the selected person was responsible for the centre, and for several paid or voluntary, full-time or part-time staff. As not all of those selected were called leaders, the title given to them in this report will be 'workers'.

Although the variety of backgrounds was hoped for, this was not taken into consideration in selection. But the variety added considerably to the learning in the project because it was possible to see the common element in the training needs of workers, amidst great differences in structure, administration and approaches. The workers gained a great deal by coming to understand that there might be similar problems in different settings; in, for example, the highly structured organised clubs and detached work. The differing values, particularly religious beliefs, provided useful experience, indicating how supervision could be used to clarify beliefs in so far as they related to work, even though they were different from each other and from those of the supervisor.

THE SEQUENCE OF TRAINING

The ten workers committed themselves to weekly training sessions for a period of twenty-one months, starting in December 1964. Apart from the facts that supervision would be the priority, that seminars would supplement training, and that practice in supervising was expected at some stage, no long term plans were made. The different stages in the training were introduced according to the apparent need and with the total length of the project in mind. At first the stages were suggested by the supervisor and agreed by the workers. As the project developed, stages were introduced following discussion based on anyone's suggestion.

From December 1964 to July 1965, workers attended individual training (supervision) sessions in the project office Because of the travelling involved, these were arranged fortnightly and lasted two hours. This appeared to be too long a period at first, and was sometimes shortened. The content of these sessions was the worker and his situation. Clubs were not visited by the supervisor – the training was based on the work as the worker saw and understood it.

On alternate weeks seminars were held, the workers dividing into two groups. They chose the subjects for discussion, and provided illustrations from their work. Much of the discussion was on different aspects of group work, but not exclusively so. The seminars were seen as a means of providing more material, theoretical and practical, to supplement individual training and to help the participants realise how much they could learn from each other and from participating in a training group. In July the seminars were discontinued for the summer, and weekly supervision was fitted in with holidays.

In September, the whole group met together for three seminars on supervision. Much of the discussion related to the participants' experience of being supervised. It was seen as the first attempt to theorise from this experience, and also, as the seminars progressed, as an introduction to the idea of supervising.

VOLUNTARY SUPERVISEES

In October 1965, eleven leaders in Greater London who had recently left college were invited to volunteer to be supervised. Six did so (at a later stage more leaders were invited, and a total of twelve were supervised). Each volunteer was interviewed by the supervisor, and except for one leader who already had a supervisor within his organisation, all were accepted. The selection here was not on suitability but on need, and it was assumed that all new leaders needed supervision. The leaders had been trained in Leicester, Westhill, and by the National Association of Boys' Clubs. They represented clubs attached to the Methodist Association of Youth Clubs, the Association of Jewish Youth, the National Association of Youth Clubs, the National Association of Boys' Clubs, two settlements, and four local authority centres.

Following the interview, and as the original workers became ready to supervise, a supervisee's (leader's) name was given to a worker, who

4

arranged a second interview with the supervisee. Both knew that the decision to continue as supervisor and supervisee would be by mutual agreement – either person could say he would prefer someone else. No one did so. The supervisor linked supervisee and worker mainly on the principle agreed by all workers that it would be helpful if supervisees were not neighbours of their supervisors, but were from another borough. Normally the supervisor first discussed the background (work) of the supervisee with the worker concerned, and also, in linking the two, noted possibilities of personality clashes. But so little was known at this stage that no one looked into these matters very deeply.

PRACTICE OF SUPERVISION

From October 1965 onwards workers continued to be supervised weekly or fortnightly, and from January 1966 met for seminars monthly. As each one became ready, he began to supervise one of the new leaders. The point at which he started followed discussion and evaluation with the supervisor, and was decided upon by mutual agreement.

Here it might be useful to distinguish between workers by giving each a letter of the alphabet, which will be used throughout the report. All supervisees will be called X as it was agreed that there would be no personal identification.

E began in October to undertake weekly supervision with a new leader. In February 1966 a leader who was in his second post asked E to supervise him. After consultation with the supervisor, and knowing he could fit two supervisees into one morning, E agreed to do so. He supervised both regularly and is still doing so (March 1967). A, B, F, G, and H were all supervising by December 1965. The supervisees of A, B and H changed their jobs in July and September 1966, and moved out of the area. Before this happened A and H had already started to supervise a second leader, and are still doing so. B decided, when taking a new job in October 1966, to wait until March 1967 before supervising again. C started to supervise in May 1966 and continues to supervise the same leader.

D and J both decided after discussion to supervise members of their own staff instead of working with professional leaders. They did so for several short periods. J decided in the autumn of 1966 to break before starting to supervise seriously in March 1967. D continued periodic supervision until he moved North in January 1967. K's first supervisee moved out of the area after his second interview in January, 1966. When another supervisee was found in April 1966, K supervised him irregularly and eventually decided not to supervise. The supervisor suggested she should continue K's supervision but the supervisee did not take up the offer.

As each worker began to supervise, so the content of his own supervision changed to a discussion of the sessions he had with his supervisee. At first some workers still continued to discuss their own work for part of the time, but this gradually became less frequent. The seminars revolved round common problems in supervising, and special seminars were held at the Child Guidance Training Centre and the University of Sussex.

THE FINAL STAGES

By May 1966, all workers agreed that they could not stop supervising when the project ended in September. They felt a responsibility towards their supervisees and did not think an abrupt end would be helpful. They also felt that the time had been too short and they had much more to learn about the skill of supervising. It was then agreed that all supervision should continue fortnightly during the period allocated to the preparation of this report (October–December 1966), and also in 1967, even if the project had then ended officially.

Meantime the Department of Education was approached to finance the project for a further period, during which the original workers could continue. In addition, training could begin for a group of youth officers, some of whom had expressed interest. It would also provide opportunities for discussions and consultations about supervision in different fields. The Department agreed to allocate a grant for another twelve months.

Eight workers continue to supervise within the project (two of these restarted in March 1967, following a break). The intervals between sessions vary according to the needs of the workers. The seminars have continued, and were used for the study of chapters of the report as each was being written. The comments of the workers, and of the supervisees who met for one evaluation session, are incorporated in the report.

THE REPORT

This report might be considered a final phase of the project. It starts with a number of assumptions on which the project was based, and from then onwards its content is taken from the experience of the project. Two points seem important in connection with this. First, the report might well have referred to material already written about adult education, learning processes, or supervision in other settings. It was decided not to do so, partly in the interests of time, and partly to ensure concentration on the learning from the project itself. A short bibliography of relevant material has been attached to the report, and it is hoped that this might be related at a later stage.

The second point is that the emphasis is not on supervision, but on supervision in youth work. The report has been prepared for those who are concerned with training in youth work, particularly supervisors or potential supervisors. This has resulted in a fairly detailed analysis of the work that was done, as it was understood. There is a risk in generalising, that an air of mystery could continue to surround supervision in youth work. There is a risk in being detailed, that supervision could appear to be over-complicated. The second risk has been taken, for it seems that, as the opportunity was given for a study of the work being done, the results should be shared as specifically as possible.

Some of the needs of youth workers arising from the youth work setting have been pin-pointed and considered alongside the training already provided. These include the particularity and structure of a worker's situation, the variety of expectations of his work, the need to understand professionalism, to relate theory and practice, and to relate different aspects of his work.

As it was assumed that training within a face-to-face relationship had a particular value, this relationship has been examined so that the factors within it could be recognised -the feelings, attitudes and expectations of the two people, the part that each played, and the way in which these affected learning. The material which workers presented for discussion in supervision indicated the areas of common need as well as individual needs. The manner of presentation also showed recognisable patterns common to all, and these have been detailed in order to show the common elements in relation to the individual approach in presenting material.

The learning of workers has been described in two ways. First, different aspects of learning have been considered – understanding theories, understanding observations, the recognition and use of feelings, the recognition and understanding of values, learning from a situation through perception and action while with people, and examination and analysis afterwards. Second, workers used supervision and approached learning in different ways, and these have been described to show some of the common elements and individual differences.

The words 'skill' and 'technique' are frequently used in the report. 'Skill' is defined as 'the practised ability to' or 'knowing how to,' and

7

'technique' as 'a method of achieving a purpose' – in this instance, to help a worker to learn and to increase his effectiveness in his work. Techniques are seen as important only in relation to other factors, which include the ability to accept the supervisee as he is, to understand his needs, to learn from him, and to relate this understanding and knowledge to the purpose of supervision. The workers/ supervisors are seen to be developing skill through understanding the supervisees and their requirements, understanding and handling their own difficulties, recognising the knowledge from which they can draw to help supervisees, practising techniques, and reflecting on all these. The particular needs of new workers are described alongside the development of skill by the supervisors. The report also describes the use of groups in complementing learning in supervision.

The criteria for evaluation are described in detail, but it must be remembered that these criteria were used only as a sounding board. Evaluation in the project was ongoing and related to the progress of an individual worker, and not his performance in relation to a set standard.

The conclusions indicate the value of supervision as a means of training, and bring the report back to the youth work setting. Suggestions are made about supervision for part-time leaders and for students, the relation between basic training and supervision, the selection and training of supervisors, the difficulties of administrators/ supervisors, the time required for supervision, and the need to consider the supervision of youth workers within a community setting.

CHAPTER TWO

Some Basic Assumptions

WHEN starting a project of this nature it was important to try to understand how far theories (about supervision) were to be applied to practice, and how far the emphasis was to be on learning from the situation. This was an experiment with two particular aims. One was 'to train leaders in the techniques of supervision in youth work' and the other 'to provide material on the nature of supervision'. Supervision in youth work was rare at this stage, which was the reason for providing material on its nature, and yet youth leaders were to be trained in its techniques. The question was, therefore, how much could be assumed as a starting point, and how much was to be learned from the experience of the project.

In the event the assumptions made related mainly to the method, or the philosophy behind the training, and were taken from the experience of supervision in the social work setting where it originated. These were then related to what was known about youth leaders and their situation. The first assumptions were as follows:

(a) That leaders on leaving college had acquired knowledge of basic theory, but lacked experience of practice as full-time youth leaders, and therefore had particular needs which called for continuation of their training during their first years in the field

(b) That the purpose of such training was to help the leader to develop his awareness of the situation in which he was working, and of his own role and behaviour within it, so that he could be relaxed and efficient in his actions; to increase his knowledge and understanding, and to apply theories so that he could base his conclusions and actions on a wide range of information, of which his own feelings were a part, but only a part

(c) That the setting in which this could most usefully take place was one in which the leader could discuss his work regularly with another person, who had no authority over him, but who was prepared to help him to learn at his own pace, and according to his own individual needs

(d) That the relationship between the two people was important in that it should create a situation in which teaching and learning were possible and fruitful. This therefore required that the leader should feel accepted, supported and significant within it, and that his confidence would be respected

(e) That the value of this method of training had been recognised in social work-casework and group work – and was already known in that setting as 'supervision'
(f) That supervision was an educational process, a form of individual adult education, in which the leader learned about the work of which he was a part
(g) That whereas the theories learnt in basic training could be related in supervision to practice, the specific content of the sessions was unknown. The needs of the leaders could be assumed, but could not be predicted on accurate evidence, and therefore the leaders would be expected to provide this information through their contributions in sessions
(h) That although the purpose of supervision could be described in general terms as helping a leader to develop his efficiency in his work, there were so many facets to his work, and such a variety of expectations in the field, that it was difficult to assume a purpose common to all leaders. The nearest generalisation was 'to help in the social development of young people'.

It must be noted here that as soon as the assumptions became related to the leader's purpose in his work they became vague, and raised an important question. Who determined the leader's purpose in his work? The basic training (six settings) did not produce a clear and mutually agreed purpose and/or methods of achieving it. Even if they had done so, the leaders were then faced with expectations of purpose and method in the field which varied between agencies and within them. The leaders therefore had to make choices as to their own purposes and approaches. This meant that although the assumption could be made that leaders would learn to be more efficient in 'helping the social development of young people', a second assumption had to be added to it – that supervision would help leaders to cope with the variety of expectations in the field, and to make useful contributions in the ongoing debate on what was meant by helping the social development of young people.

As the project had as an objective the training of leaders in the techniques of supervision, there were other assumptions. The specific nature of supervision in youth work, as compared with general theories about it, was yet to be worked out, and the project was arranged so that some aspects of supervision could be understood before the leaders began to practise supervising. But there was a more important reason for this arrangement – the need for experience of being supervised before supervising. The assumptions behind this were:

(a) That leaders should have an opportunity of meeting their own needs in learning about their work, before being asked to meet the needs of other leaders, and also that they needed to understand the meaning of learning from a situation

(b) That the experience of the supervisory relationship, in which they were accepted and supported without sentiment, would help leaders to understand how they could help and support another leader in a similar way

(c) That experience of being supervised would help leaders in their understanding of the attitudes, feelings and behaviour of their own supervisees.

Knowing that the leaders being supervised were learning to supervise, meant that the project supervisor made two other assumptions about her work in the project. First, she assumed that, when supervising in the early stages, she would not only be helping the leaders to become more efficient in their work, but would be seeing them as potential supervisors. This meant that she would spend time helping them to become aware of what was happening in supervision, and that she would have to take care that such awareness was encouraged at points where it would help a leader's learning and not hinder it. It also meant a slightly different emphasis in learning, for there was a difference between helping a leader to be more effective in his own work and helping him to take on a completely different role. These thoughts were noted but their implications were not fully understood at this stage.

The second assumption was that, although at first the supervisor had the main responsibility for the project, and for interpreting it publicly in so far as this was possible, a main objective was for participants to accept increasing responsibility so that before the end of the period it would become a team project, in which everyone shared responsibility for programme and for interpretation. It was also expected that seminars for the participants would supplement the individual training and help leaders to realise how much they could learn from each other and from group participation. But there was the additional assumption that working as a group would accelerate the process of shared responsibility, and that the group would support each individual in the transition from supervisee to supervisor. This would also mean that the group could eventually replace the project supervisor as a support.

OTHER FACTORS

These assumptions were derived from previous experience and theoretical considerations. The other important assumption therefore was that the project itself would provide new learning, new understanding and new skill. In other words, not only were the leaders to learn from their own situations, but it was expected that the project would provide a situation from which leaders and supervisor would learn, and be able to analyse and explain that which had been learned.

The project was started with all these factors in mind, though not all were clearly defined. There were also minor hidden assumptions of which no one was fully aware at that stage.

CHAPTER THREE

Supervision in a Youth Work Setting

ONE of the basic assumptions made was that youth workers have particular needs which call for a continuation of their training during their first years in the field. Although some of these are individual because of a worker's temperament or inexperience, there are a number which arise from the setting in which he works, the youth service, and it is the latter which are described in this chapter.

SUPERVISION AND OTHER TRAINING

There are already several types of help available to a new youth worker. Youth officers are available to introduce a worker to his new job, to explain administration and give advice and help where needed. Management committees are responsible for supporting workers and working out policies with them. Colleagues in the field provide opportunities for sharing experiences, problems and ideas. Short training courses are arranged at intervals to cover particular aspects of youth work. It is generally recognised, however, that the value and potential of this help varies from area to area, from individual to individual, and that they frequently have to be set against the clashes which arise from differences in expectations and temperaments. But even though increased understanding is widespread, and attempts are being made to increase facilities and opportunities, at least one gap remains – a worker is rarely able to find a continuity of training which will help him to understand his own work and how all its aspects are related. Supervision could be seen as one answer.

Supervision as a form of training was started in the social casework setting, and has since been used as a recognised part of training in social group work. The introduction of social group work to full-time youth leadership training in England, naturally brought with it the possibility that supervision would also be valuable. To those who saw training in social group work as a cure for all ills in youth service, supervision would have as its content, social group work. But because of the present nature of full-time youth work in England, if supervision is to help a worker to increase his understanding and effectiveness in his work, it must include, among other aspects, social group work, educational work, the training of adults, administration, co-operation in the community, and the understanding of the structure within which he works.

While to many people this might seem obvious, it indicates the function of supervision, not only in supporting a worker and helping him understand his work more clearly, but also in helping him to acquire new knowledge and skill. For example, in the basic courses, workers are trained mainly in working with young people, although many other aspects of the work may be included. But the courses are of too short a duration to allow adequate time for a worker to learn how to train the adults with whom he works, in addition to co-operating with them. Yet this is normally an essential part of a worker's job. Supervision can therefore be seen not only as a help to the worker during transition from college to work, but also as a continuation of training through helping a worker to acquire new knowledge and develop new skills.

A PARTICULAR STRUCTURE

Perhaps the most important need of a worker is to understand the particular structure in which he is working and the different functions within that structure. The ways in which people relate to each other, policies and purposes, the allocation of authority, are just a few of the factors which vary from centre to centre, from organisation to organisation, and from local authority to local authority.

Whereas it seems comparatively easy in academic training to teach some of the common elements – in human relations, individual and group behaviour, committee work, differences between adolescents and adults, social structure – it is perhaps impossible to teach a student the nature of a particular structure, and how to work within it. When a worker leaves college he is confronted by a situation in which he must find his level. One generalisation frequently heard is that a youth leader works within the policy of an agency or organisation and understands what this is before taking up an appointment. But what happens if national policy is quite different from local policy? What happens if 'enlightened' officials of an organisation are trying to get a management committee to change its ideas? What happens if a worker, trained to help his members to take responsibility and make their own decisions, finds himself in an authoritarian centre although this is denied by the management committee? What happens if he is involved in the difference between lip-service and behaviour, between behaviour and attitudes? If he is not to be blown by the wind and utterly frustrated, he needs to know how to navigate within the structure in which he finds himself. It could be said that all this falls in the area of human relationships – but it is also about purpose, roles, concepts, and procedures, and how they link up with structures and functions.

For some workers, an understanding of a particular structure was a most important part of learning within supervision. There were at least three aspects to be considered. First he had to understand how all individuals and groups in his work related to each other, the parts they played, their powers and peculiarities. Second he had to understand the part he must play in relation to all of these, and where he could change, be changed or compromise. Third, and this in part resulted from the first two, he had to learn to live with that which existed. 'If only there were no management committee, I could get on with my job.' 'If only the youth officer wouldn't insist on activities.' 'If only voluntary helpers would come regularly.' Since these comments said a lot about the structure, they and similar thoughts had to disappear through increased awareness, understanding and action. Here then in such a complicated youth service, supervision has an important part to play in supplementing college training – the structure can be understood only by examination, over a long period, of incidents, situations, feelings, values, relationships and purposes.

A PROFESSIONAL WORKER

Another important factor is that new leaders need help in understanding what it means to be a professional worker. The basic concept that many workers have is that being trained means that one has been made professional. Added to this is a belief that the professional is the knowledgeable person who knows better than the lay person and can teach him. But the workers are vague as to the areas of knowledge which can be taught. Also they suggest that they should behave in certain ways, that is, professionally, respecting confidence, or being non-judgemental, but they are not always clear how to behave in these ways.

Youth leadership as a profession is comparatively new, and the elements of behaviour which make it professional require experience and an examination of that experience, before they can be fully understood and agreed upon by the workers themselves. But meantime, being a new profession, youth workers want recognition, and sometimes need to struggle for it. Difficulties appear to arise when workers cannot wait to get recognition on the basis of the work which they do, but hope to get it from the fact that they are trained and from a statement of principles which they do not fully understand. Employers and others in a community can vary between expecting a worker to know what must be done because he is trained (which sometimes means expecting him to know what the employers think should be done), and waiting to see what he does before recognising him as a responsible person. With all these factors, and others, professionalism is liable to have a thorny passage, and a first essential is that workers should understand through experience what they believe.

The reality of transition from student to professional worker was first indicated in the project when workers were asked to attend supervisory sessions away from their clubs, which were not being visited by the supervisor. It was recognised that they were responsible to their employing bodies. The supervisory function (while sometimes helping them in relation to their employers) was not to see that they did their work properly, but to help them understand their work at the points at which the workers indicated that they needed help. The decisions as to what help and training he required was the worker's responsibility, although the supervisor was prepared to help him understand what he required.

The acceptance of this responsibility by the worker was sometimes a slow process, but through it he was helped to do his own thinking and to accept the consequences of his own actions. He had to look at his situation, consider what he was doing and how he felt about it, and learn to describe and analyse it. In time professionalism took on a new meaning, based on his own behaviour and his situation, in relation to the theory he had learned in college. One worker said after twelve months, 'I knew I was a professional worker but I didn't know what it meant. Sometimes I thought it meant becoming more and more remote and suppressing my personality. Now, I am beginning to realise that it is about specific actions – it is a mixture of observation, awareness, thinking, action, and skills, and my personality is involved in these!' Exploration of the responsibility undertaken and of other people's attitudes to it is therefore a second area where supervision can help in the transition from college to full-time appointments.

THEORY AND PRACTICE

The third area which seems important is that of understanding theory through practice. Terminology itself can be a stumbling block. Some words have been taught and are used, but have not been fully grasped. 'Social interaction', 'confidentiality', 'group identity', 'supervision', 'equality' are some of the terms which can be used easily but not explained, and this means that communications can be affected immediately. Similarly, phrases are apparently understood but not in terms of people. It is easy to accept that one should 'help people in their relationships', but not so easy to know how to apply this knowledge when confronted by a group. Also, some parts of theory can be remembered and others forgotten, so that one might remember to 'draw out leadership' when working with a group, and forget the numerous other functions of a worker with a group. The situation, and the people in front of him, can almost paralyse a new worker's thinking, so that on occasions he rejects the theory he has learned and returns to that which he understood before college - and worries about the consequences. Supervision can provide support to a worker while he is observing human behaviour, situations and himself, and finding his own words to describe and analyse it. It can help him to relate theories and understand more technical language, at appropriate moments, so that they give new meaning to practice, and can be used to help communication instead of hindering it.

PRIORITIES AND PATTERN

Another area in which workers frequently need help is in the use of time, in determining priorities, and in relating the different parts of their work. A new worker has good reason to believe that he must assess needs, work with individuals and groups and negotiate between groups, develop interests, help relationships, help young people to mature and fit into society, work in the community, co-operate with the youth officer, youth leaders, probation officer, employment officer, social workers, teachers, parents, support the professional body, carry out the requirements of the management committee, train volunteers and part-time workers, help in training courses – and don't forget administration! Inevitably the worker must make choices, and sometimes the choice is based on 'what lies to hand', 'what the management committee wants', or 'what I can do most competently'. The difficulties arise when numerous demands are made, and the problem which emerges is 'time'. New possibilities in the job are frequently considered in terms of time and it becomes difficult to see any pattern in the work. 'If I had no administration, I could think about members' needs.' 'Once I get the activities organised I can think about group work.' Perhaps the most basic need of a new worker is to get help in relating these parts of his job so that he can make choices within a total pattern.

In supervision a worker can find help in observing and examining each aspect of his work in terms of people or situations, and then gradually in relating one aspect to another, until they become recognisable, acceptable and manageable as a total job. Although supervision is only one small part of training, it is possible that if training could be seen as an ongoing process within a total programme, the particular function of supervision could be to provide the opportunity for a worker to look intensively at his own job, himself in it, and its relation to the community in which it exists. This is perhaps its fundamental value, and can result in a more mature self-confidence which is able to use, participate in, and initiate the advice and training facilities described at the beginning of this chapter.

CHAPTER FOUR

The Supervisory Relationship

DEFINING A RELATIONSHIP

THE assumption on which this chapter is based is that the relationship between the two people concerned – the supervisor and supervisee – plays an important part in the teaching/learning process. In order to establish this point, the use of the word relationship needs to be clarified, and then explored within a supervisory setting.

Two definitions of relationship seem important within this context. The first is that a relationship is 'the way in which one person is thought of in connection with another' and the second, 'association between persons'. Within these definitions are four aspects. First, there are (at least) two persons in the relationship, each with thoughts and feelings about the other. Second, it can be seen (presumably by participants and/or onlookers) that the connection between the two people is of a particular kind, which results in people talking of a 'mother/child relationship' a 'sexual relationship', or a 'professional relationship'. Third, the definitions imply that the two persons are in contact with each other, exchanging ideas, giving and taking, talking and listening. Fourth, they indicate movement, that a relationship is not static, but that changes as well as exchanges are taking place. In order to explore a relationship, therefore, at least four factors have to be considered – two persons in contact, two persons giving to and taking from each other, the particular nature of the contact and exchange, and the possibilities of change.

TWO PERSONS WITH FEELINGS, ATTITUDES EXPECTATIONS

As we move into the supervisory relationship it seems appropriate to begin with the two persons concerned. Who are they? How do they feel? What are their attitudes and expectations? The supervisee in this instance is the worker who was accepted as a worker with potential for supervising other workers, and the supervisor is the person who accepted responsibility for training workers to supervise. Later we shall consider the similarities and differences between these and new workers and supervisors.

The first workers came into the project with feelings of gratification for which there were several reasons. They had been selected from numerous applicants, which meant that they were seen to be effective in their work. To some this was confirmation of their own understanding of themselves, to others it brought an element of surprise which added to their pleasure. Another reason was that while there was a growing demand for further training there was very little opportunity for it. Acceptance for the project brought with it a certain amount of status, recognition, and the possibility of contributing to the youth service in a different way. All these factors contributed, towards making the workers pleased with themselves and with the idea of being supervised.

Several workers also felt relief at the prospect of being supervised. They had been out of college for two years, and although they could point to achievements in their work, they also realised that they needed help in it. Some could locate the areas in which they required help. Others had become confused and wanted help in sorting out the confusion. They hoped that supervision would be helpful, and were relieved that this opportunity had come their way.

Feelings of gratification and relief were pleasant. But supervision also presented a new situation. Apart from brief periods in college, only one worker had experienced being supervised. Although assumptions could be made about it, supervision and the relationship within it were unknown territory. The feelings aroused by this ranged through curiosity, interest, excitement, unease, apprehension and fear. It is probable that most workers experienced all these feelings at some point, but the strength of each feeling varied from person to person. A worker wondered if he would be able to learn at the required pace, or feared what would happen to him if he didn't. He was uneasy about what would go on between himself and the supervisor, or apprehensive about the discovery of his weaknesses. It seemed that the uncomfortable feelings were due to not knowing what would happen, and concern about inadequacy and failure.

It was inevitable that feelings, both pleasant and uncomfortable, should move towards the supervisor and affect the workers' attitudes towards her. Workers saw in supervision opportunities to get help, to learn, to get recognition, and they also thought that someone had to see that these things happened. Workers were prepared to work, but at the time the importance of the relationship itself was not understood, so that the main responsibility for success was put on to the supervisor. Workers wanted to be sure the supervisor was known to be adequate for the task. The only known fact to support this was that she had been asked to do it. One worker commented that she had not previously heard of the supervisor. Another quickly pointed out that she was known in other circles. So her status had to be established. Then the workers wanted her to be knowledgeable. This could not be assessed at first sight, but such was their need for help and success that some workers expected her to be, and made her, the knowledgeable authority. Their attitude was that she must be 'right', and if they objected to a comment or method, they must be wrong. This meant that negative feelings towards the supervisor were denied, and workers tried to please her. So questions asked were: 'Is this what you want?', 'Was this information helpful to you?'. Some workers who did not feel so strongly, or perhaps who had feelings equally strong which tended to make them resist an authority, could present their material more firmly and reserved their judgement.

Uncomfortable feelings were also present. just as the supervisor was seen to be largely responsible for the success of the enterprise, so she was seen as responsible for what would happen to the workers. So their attitudes were questioning. Can she be trusted? Will she gossip about me to officials or colleagues? What will she expect of me? Will she tell me what to do, or give me advice, and if neither of these things, what can she do? The uncomfortable feelings sent unspoken questions to the supervisor – questions as to her integrity, her emotional reactions, her skill and her expectations. Thus, it can be seen that the desire for good and profitable experience, together with concern about the unknown, produced conflicting feelings which affected the attitudes of the workers, and contributed to their expectations of the parts they and the supervisor would play within the relationship.

The supervisor too had feelings both pleasant and uncomfortable. She was pleased at the opportunity to do this job for several reasons. Supervision as a method of training was being discussed in the youth service – it was being accepted, questioned, or resisted. The supervisor believed it to be valuable to workers and wanted to prove it. Secondly, she wished to learn more about it so that she could understand more clearly what it involved. Thirdly, she enjoyed training workers and was glad of the opportunity to do so without being concerned with administrative work.

The supervisor's uncomfortable feelings were about the unknown. Would the London Council of Social Service or colleagues pressure her for results or evidence of success? Would the workers be pressured in the same way? Would she be able to help them handle such pressures? Had she selected wisely? Knowing that she believed in this method of helping and training workers, would she be able to carry it out by being sufficiently receptive and flexible to enable workers to supervise according to their own understanding and skill ? These questions were related to the pressures and the responsibility for an experiment as well as concern about her own skill.

At this point the way in which the supervisor's feelings affected the relationship differed in part from those of the workers. The nature of the job she had undertaken necessitated recognition and management of her own feelings, so that they were not directed towards the worker. If she worried about pressures for results and didn't know she was doing so, or didn't know how this might affect her attitudes and expectations, inevitably she would affect the worker as he too would feel pressured. She had to try to understand her feelings, recognise what they could do, and then concentrate on helping the worker. Again, part of her job was to know some of her expectations and attitudes with regard to the worker. She already expected that workers would have some of these feelings, attitudes and expectations. But she also realised that she would not know them all, and that she would have to observe, listen and think, in order to understand what workers were feeling, saying, thinking and expecting. The basic factor was that she knew the feelings were there, but she did not know their extent or form – these were particular to the individual. So she too had to ask herself questions about the workers. These, together with those of the workers, could only be answered by the ongoing contact and exchange.

THE NATURE OF THE RELATIONSHIP AND THE EXCHANGES

The exchanges between the two persons which were mainly verbal were dependent on the feelings, attitudes and expectations of one person towards the other, as already described, and as they changed through continuing contact. Second, they were dependent on the understanding by both persons of the nature and purpose of the relationship, and the part each was prepared or able to play in order to achieve this. It is this second aspect which now needs to be considered.

The supervisory relationship existed for the purpose of training. Basically it consisted of two professional workers who met together, and whose exchanges were about work. Through the exchanges the supervisor helped the worker to learn – to understand himself better in his job, to become more competent, and to understand how to supervise.

The supervisor's ititial responsibility

The supervisor took the responsibility for clarifying the nature and purpose of the relationship, and for helping the workers to understand it and to use it. Initially she felt that it was her task to explain what the exchanges would be about. She recognised some of the feelings in the workers, particularly those concerned with the unknown, the 'mystery', and decided that in some measure they could be relieved by explanation. The main points explained were that the sessions were to help the worker to learn more about his work and himself in it, and that for this to happen they would need to explore the areas in his work in which the worker wanted help or needed to understand more. This meant that the material discussed would be brought to sessions by the worker and would be about his work. The supervisor would help him to look at what he was doing, to think about it and to learn about it. She had no authority over him, nor would she be asked to produce any report about his work. The material for the report of the project would be agreed by him before it was published. He would begin to practise supervising when they both agreed he was ready. This, in brief, was the nature of the explanation though was it given as part of a discussion, and was therefore in itself the beginning of verbal exchanges in the relationship. Some workers understood it and were reassured, some understood parts of it, others who were more anxious probably did not hear or could not remember most of it. Even the understanding had little meaning, for it was in outline, and the details had to be filled in by later discussion and experience.

Three misconceptions emerged very quickly. Some workers did not understand how to start a relationship through exchanges about work - or found it difficult to do so. They began with social chat, or invited the supervisor for tea. It seemed they believed that, if they could get to know the supervisor socially, they might be able to work together. The supervisor felt it unwise to accept the social relationship when it was used as a substitute for a working relationship, or if it blocked a worker's understanding of the possibilities within one. When the working relationship was established and being used to achieve its purpose, social contacts were seen as acceptable, but by that time they were no longer so important to the worker.

Other misconceptions were that exchanges would be about the personality of the worker – that his conscious and unconscious would be carefully explored; or that the relationship would be problem centred, and the supervisor was there to help workers solve their problems. Workers could not see what would happen if they had none.

The supervisor had to emphasise the work-centred nature of the relationship and show that she was neither psychiatrist nor caseworker, and they were neither patients nor people in distress. Thus, in clarifying the nature and purpose of the relationship and trying to sort out misconceptions, the supervisor was determining her first function - an acceptance of responsibility.

The supervisor's understanding of her other functions

The supervisor's responsibility also included taking on the role of teacher in the context of teacher/learner relationship. She believed this to mean that she must:

get to know the worker – learn about him and his situation,
support him in his situation,
accept the worker as he was,
help the worker to learn.

The supervisor was therefore to learn, support, accept and help.

First, then, the supervisor was the learner – she wanted to know what kind of person the worker was, how he felt about his work, how he carried out his responsibilities, what he understood, what he wanted to understand, what his club and total working situation were like. She also wanted to learn how he saw their relationship, what he was prepared to give to it and take from it. She could learn these things only gradually by observing the worker and listening to him, and the learning, observation and listening continued throughout the relationship.

Secondly, the supervisor was supporting – supporting the worker in his situation; no matter what he said and did, no matter how misguided he might appear to be in her eyes, her function was a supporting one – he was the person she was to help, so she had to understand how he felt at that moment and let him know that she understood that he felt that way. Several workers used the relationship in the first instance to grumble about the youth service and pour out bottled-up grievances. Her function was neither to agree nor disagree but to recognise that they were finding life difficult. Sometimes the support was given in relation to a worker's own learning or his inability to learn because of pressures on the job. The supervisor had to let the worker see that she understood that this aspect of learning was difficult for him, or cooperate in a more relaxing discussion. The supporting function was needed less frequently as the relationship developed, but there were occasions - new situations or crises - when it was required again.

Thirdly, the supervisor was accepting – accepting that the worker was a person with feelings and attitudes and expectations, that he was a professional worker doing a job, and knew more about that particular job than she did, that he had strengths and weaknesses, ideals and frustrations, skills, knowledge and integrity, and that his responsibilities were to his employers, colleagues, members and community. He was doing his own job according to his own understanding and ability – her function was not to try to make him do it as she would do it. He was responsible to other people – her function was not to exert authority over him. He had his own personality, values, strengths and weaknesses – her function was not to disapprove, sympathise with him or laugh at him. Her function was to accept that which the worker was and could do at any given moment. This was more difficult to establish at the beginning, and contrary to supporting, became more acceptable as the relationship developed. At first the workers wanted a new authority (presumably sometimes to resist it), wanted to know the opinions and values of the supervisor with regard to themselves and their jobs, and although they didn't want ridicule, they wanted sympathy and approval. It was sometimes hard for the supervisor to maintain the accepting function under pressures from the workers, but when they began to understand the relationship, and gain confidence in themselves, they welcomed it.

The supervisor was also helping – helping the worker to learn. The learning covered a wide area, but basically it included the worker's understanding of his work and of what he was feeling, thinking and doing about it, his finding points at which he wanted to change and learn, discovering new factors he could learn about, understanding the supervisory relationship, and acquiring skills in supervising. In accepting, the supervisor was also accepting that the workers themselves were not content as they were – which was why they had joined the project. In helping, she was concerned with their movement from where they were to where they wanted to be – supervisors. To this end she was concerned with helping the worker to understand the contributions that he and the supervisor could make in the relationship, so that the two together could look at the material – the worker in his job – and so that the relationship could be one in which learning was pos sible. Finally the supervisor was helping the worker to a point where he no longer needed or wanted the relationship, but would continue to learn without it.

The supervisor therefore had basic assumptions as to what her functions would be – learning, supporting, accepting and helping – and by her behaviour had to help the workers understand that these were the ways in which she was prepared to give to the relationship. The supervisor's use of different functions depended sometimes on the worker's expressed need, and sometimes on her understanding or assumption of his need, but always it was in relation to the needs of the individual worker at any given moment. Sometimes she misjudged the need or misjudged the moment. The following four examples are of the supervisor's functions in relation to the worker's expectation and need.

EXAMPLE I

A brought a record to the session and said, 'Will you tell me if this is a good record?'

S Do you think it is good?
A I don't know. That is why I am asking.
S What do you mean by good?
A Useful.
S Useful to whom?
A Useful to me, I think.
S Was it useful?
A Writing it seemed to clear my thoughts about the members, but otherwise I didn't know how I could use it.
S Suppose we look at it to find out?

The record was then explored.

Comment

A wanted S to judge his work, and saw this to be a way in which she could help him. S did not see this as her function as she thought she should help him to be his own judge. A co-operated in this.

EXAMPLE 2

(First session). B said she didn't know what to expect in supervision, that she was in a muddle, and didn't know where she was going at all. S asked if she could describe some of the things that were happening. B said she was inundated with volunteers, referred to her because they needed help - she had nine in an evening and couldn't cope. Then followed a description of the background, structure and programme of the centre. B sounded upset and was fairly critical throughout. S agreed that it sounded a very complicated situation. She asked: 'What can you do about it?' B looked taken aback by this question but after a moment said she supposed she could resign, though she had tried this once and hadn't gone through with it. With questioning, B suggested that two other alternatives were: going on in a muddle and accepting it, or trying to understand what was happening and taking some action to improve matters.

Comment

B wasn't sure what kind of help she wanted though she sounded as if she might want a shoulder to cry on. She was unprepared for the suggestion that she might help herself, but did so in the session and accepted the help offered. S saw her function as showing that she understood that B had problems, and then helping her to see that she could take some action, and that there were choices.

EXAMPLE 3

C commented that she found It difficult to know what to discuss. Everything was going smoothly; she could now understand what was happening in the club, and had learned quite a lot about groups. S reminded C of an earlier comment about supervision, and asked if she meant that she no longer wanted or needed it. C said no, she liked coming to talk things over. S said they could probably go on having a cosy chat, but that C had now been having supervision for some time – it could be a waste of C's time if she didn't know what she wanted to learn from it. C thought she did want to learn but didn't know what. S suggested that the time might have come for some disciplined thought about it. If she felt confident and at case in her work, perhaps she could start recording as an exercise in learning, or perhaps she could begin to supervise and use these sessions to learn about her supervision. C considered this and then said she knew she had avoided recording because of the time involved, but she also knew that she should make the effort. S suggested that C might think about it during the week and make her choice.

Comment

C had reached a point where nothing In her surroundings was stimulating her to go on learning. She knew this and expressed it. S acted as a stimulus.

EXAMPLE 4

D described a camping expedition, then a staff conference and group methods used there. He went on to give his ideas for a staff training day which he was planning, and then described the programme of a senior members' group. He then talked about problems with other leaders. All of this was given in some detail and lasted nearly an hour. Eventually D slowed down and stopped. There was silence for five minutes, then S asked, 'Are you ready to go?'

D No, I am wondering actually.
S What are you wondering?
D I am wondering what you are up to. You are not asking questions as you usually do.
S I am wondering at this point how I can be helpful to you.
D It is helpful to be able to talk. I find that as I go on talking I can think more about what to do, and I am becoming clearer.
S Does this mean you want a sounding board?
D No, I want you to ask questions.
S Where would you like me to ask them?
D (after some thought) I don't know.

S   You have described five different situations. Each one is interesting but how am I to judge which one you want to think about? Don't you think it is time you made your own decisions about this?

D   Yes, I get your point (after thought). I really want to discuss the training day.

Comment

D found it useful to talk about his work, but left it to S to decide which subject was to be discussed. S had, in part, accepted this previously but thought it was probably not helping. She changed to being listener, with which D was not satisfied. D expressed dissatisfaction and challenged what S was doing. It was then possible to discuss her function, which resulted in D making a different contribution.

UNDERSTANDING THE RELATIONSHIP

These examples are of isolated incidents, used to demonstrate functions in relation to needs and attitudes. Obviously one session alone included many incidents, and it is only when a number are seen together that they can be understood as determining a pattern in a relationship. The following illustration indicates the beginning of such a pattern. It describes E's first three sessions in supervision, and an attempt has been made to describe the functions and attitudes of the two people, and their learning about each other and the relationship. The records are summarised.

EXAMPLE 5

FIRST SESSION

E immediately started to talk about youth work generally, and then described his centre and his work within it in some detail. He talked of proposed developments and the appointment of new staff He also explained the relation between the centre and other clubs in the area, his relations with the youth officer and the other leaders, and his management committee. He sounded as if he enjoyed his work and felt confident within it, though he sounded a little remote. S made little comment, but occasionally asked questions for clarification.

SECOND SESSION

Again E opened the session by talking about his centre, and the variety of groups within it. He described a large 'tough' group that had joined, how the 'respectable' and the 'tough' were influencing each other, and how he had introduced the 'tough' group to helping old people. S again made little comment. E then produced his notes of a meeting of a members' committee which had been difficult. He described what had happened with regard to the business of the meeting. S asked if he had noticed anything else happening in the committee, but E could not think of anything. At S's suggestion, both then discussed the participation of the members in getting the business through. S asked several questions to help E see that participation and business could be related. E saw his own role only as helping the business along. S then asked about his participation in committees on which he served, and E described his attitudes and feelings about them. He seemed a little dismayed to realise that there were factors in the committee meetings which he had not already recognised. He then talked about his ideas for members' training.

E started by saying he would begin with a problem. He described some of the difficulties of the 'tough' group in relation to the old people. S asked several questions, and from E's answers it became increasingly obvious that he thought he knew what to do and had already taken action. S continued the discussion and then said, 'You seem to know what you are doing'. E went on to describe his work with a student group. He then said he had been asked to train volunteers in leadership and didn't know how to start. S suggested he should think how he might start. E decided he would ask an individual in the group what he thought a leader should be like. S asked how the individual might feel. E thought for a minute and then said, 'embarrassed'. He then said he supposed he could ask the whole group. The discussion on this led to S suggesting they might consider why the volunteers were there. E said 'to learn'.

S Why do they want to learn?
E To be better leaders, or because they are not sure of themselves − or have problems.
S Do you think they might be interested in learning through a discussion of problems they are facing?
E Yes, I think they might—problems can be a good point for beginning to learn.
S That doesn't mean one has to create problems in order to learn though does it?
E laughed and said; 'No, I realise that now'.

Comment

In these first three sessions, several things were happening in the relationship. Both behaved in certain ways, and learned something about their own behaviour, the behaviour of the other, and some things they might expect from the other. To an extent their original feelings, attitudes and expectations were being modified or changed by these early contacts.

E'S BEHAVIOUR, AND HIS LEARNING ABOUT S AND THE RELATIONSHIP

E, knowing that supervision was to be about his work, presented to S a picture of the work as he saw it. He was prepared to talk as long as S listened. When S took the initiative in the second session and asked him to look more deeply into what he was describing, E co-operated, but was not too happy to find that in co-operating he had been made to think about something he didn't already know. So he changed the subject to that which he did know. In the third session E tested S by producing as a problem a situation he understood and with which he could deal. After S had discussed it as presented, he produced a different problem, and co-operated in looking at it. He laughed at his action in presenting the first problem.

At the end of these sessions E had learned that in the relationship he could contribute, could talk about his work and S would listen; he could change a subject and S would accept it; S would probably accept any material he presented, but might sometimes press him to look at what he was saying; they could co-operate in a discussion; S was not easily misled; if he revealed that he didn't know what to do, S would merely help him to try to find out. He had also learned some things about S as a person from the way she had talked or from gestures. He probably felt that he had shown he was competent and intelligent, and having established this had been able to reveal one or two inadequacies and had learned from doing so. He had probably felt at ease most of the time, and uneasy on occasions. It is unlikely that E was aware of all these things at the time, though he might have become aware of some between sessions. But he was beginning to understand the behaviour he might expect from the supervisor, and what each could give and take in the relationship.

S's BEHAVIOUR, AND HER LEARNING ABOUT E

S was aware that she had been asking herself questions about E throughout the sessions, and this in part had determined her behaviour. She wanted to know how he felt, how he spoke, how he saw his job, his strengths, points at which he wanted to learn, his insights, attitudes and expectations. So she spent much of the time listening.

S learned that E spoke easily and well; that he relaxed when he described his work, and seemed to enjoy it, and to be confident about it; that he was a person of ideas, was probably a good organiser and could get things done; that he could probably get on well with adults, and wanted to make progress professionally; that he cared about people, and didn't appear to have prejudices about types of members; that he was perhaps more concerned with tasks to be done than with relationships between people; that he might find difficulty in getting involved with people and in understanding how they felt and how he felt; that his understanding of group work was not clear. In considering these possibilities, S thought E might also, in supervision, try to concentrate on the task to be done, and see S in a role similar to the one he took in his work. S could see that E was prepared to give material to the discussion, to ask for help and to think about what both said, and that he liked intellectual discussions. She realised that she would have to would have to be careful not to be drawn into intellectual discussions, which she might enjoy, but which would not necessarily help.

S tested out E's ability to learn, first by questioning what he was saying about the committee. She realised that he had been uncomfortable, but could probably cope with increased awareness. She saw in some vague way that his difficulties about feelings were connected with his professional role, as he could describe how he felt in other situations.

S's response to E's testing out was to discuss a non-existent problem as though it were a real one, as she believed that E should choose his own material and learn from it. She brought the situation into the open later, because she thought the relationship had changed.

At this stage S could not know that her knowledge of E was accurate. She had made deductions based on his behaviour, and those would have to be set alongside new learning in later sessions. (On reading this example, E pointed out that there had been a real problem underlying his presentation of an apparently non-existent problem. He had been worried about the action he had taken, and the discussion had released the tension about it. Neither E nor S was aware of this at the time.) But at this stage the deductions were the only guide lines to help S contribute and know what could be done together in this particular relationship. They were not always made in the sessions – frequently they emerged when a session was recorded. The time between sessions and the reflections that followed was therefore affecting the contacts.

SUMMARY
S and E were giving and taking throughout the sessions, and as they did so they were learning what each was prepared to offer and to take. The exchanges were specific, but they resulted in work being done together, and they were the foundations on which the relationship would grow.

THE CHANGING RELATIONSHIP
Inevitably, the relationship between supervisor and worker was changing all the time. The feelings, attitudes and expectations affected the behaviour of the two people (the nature of the exchanges), and in turn, the behaviour affected the feelings and expectations. This continued throughout the period of the relationship, but as one learned more about the other, and as each understood the parts that could be played, so the relationship developed a stability resulting from a mutual understanding of its possibilities.

This development meant that the relationship went through different phases. The time one phase lasted, and the time taken to change from one phase to another, varied from worker to worker, but phases could always be identified.

The first phase, as described earlier, was a period of getting to know each other, of understanding what each person had to offer, and what each could take. To some, this was a new kind of relationship, so this period was mainly one of testing out. Even though the workers were learning about themselves in their work throughout this phase, they were also giving time to learning about and understanding the relationship. For most workers it lasted for about eight sessions. About this time, the supervisor suggested to workers that they might in one session evaluate supervision by describing what they understood supervision to be, how it had helped or not helped, and any differences it had made to their work. Each worker did so, and many of their comments were about the relationship – the difference between their first expectations and the reality, the supervisor's role, and their own feelings and contributions.

Some comments were that supervising was not overseeing, giving answers, chipping in, criticising, disapproving or reassuring; that it was being aware of what was being said, understanding, listening, knowing when to speak, being a mirror. Workers talked of feeling supported and encouraged, of being able to think, to communicate, to express themselves, of missing advice, and of not being spoonfed. One said: 'It's a unique situation really, a collective relationship', and another: 'It's a face-to-face situation. There's no way out. One has to face up to it.' For many workers, this was the first time that functions and feelings had been put into words and clarified in a session. It resulted in their being more relaxed, able to spend less time in wondering what was happening in the relationship, and able to concentrate more on using the relationship to learn about their work and themselves in it.

The second phase therefore was one in which it was easier to learn and to concentrate on learning. The contributions within the relationship were more easily understood, and gradually behaviour became more predictable. A worker might say: 'I know what you are going to say', or 'Wait, I want to work this out'. Silences became comfortable, and expressions sometimes replaced words about something mutually understood. But most important of all, there was little concentration on the relationship itself – it was merely being used to help the two people look outwards to the job the worker was doing. Together they looked at the material brought by the worker – his work and himself in it. This phase lasted for most of the project, and became increasingly fruitful in terms of learning, as it developed. Even so, this phase was not entirely one of smooth progression – there were other developments in the relationship.

From time to time, there were periods when a worker became dependent on the supervisor. This happened at times of crisis, when a worker lost his job, or when he entered a new situation, such as a new job, or supervising, or when the variety of expectations about the work created apparent chaos. At these times the growing strength of the relationship made it possible for workers to say what they really felt and were worried about. They knew that they would not only get support, but were in a situation where they could think more clearly about the difficulties and get help in doing so. More than one worker commented: 'Supervision seems to be the only thing that is stable just now.'

Occasionally workers became more dependent when they were trying to understand and change some aspect of their own behaviour. To most workers, insights into their own behaviour developed fairly easily along with insights into other aspects of the job. But sometimes it was more difficult, and was a struggle over a long period. It was because of the nature of the relationship that a worker felt free to work out what might be preventing him from behaving in his centre as he wanted to behave, and he leaned on the supervisor as he did so.

In most instances, periods when a worker was more dependent lasted only for a short time, and gradually they became less frequent and ever shorter. Normally they were accepted and understood by the worker, but not always. One worker did not come to several sessions, at a time when he wanted help but also wanted to be independent of help. Two other workers were worried about becoming too dependent. One put it into words: 'I am worried in case I shall not be able to manage without supervision'. The supervisor tried to recognise this anxiety, whether or not it was put into words. She reminded a worker of other situations he had come through, of other areas of work in which he was independent. Her objective was to reassure him, not by saying that he would soon be self-reliant again, but by helping him to know for himself that this would happen.

But also, in recognising a temporary need for dependence, the supervisor had to be sure that she was offering the kind of support which would help a worker towards self-reliance and restore the balance in the relationship. When a worker had come through a difficulty of this kind, he was not only aware of another possibility in the relationship, but was usually able to learn about other aspects of his work at an increased pace. The second phase was thus one of growing mutual understanding in which the main purpose of the relationship was being achieved, but it was also one in which feelings could be expressed and changes occurred according to need.

The final phase in the relationship was a movement towards the time when workers no longer needed help through supervision, but could continue their learning and develop skill without it. It should have been a natural progression, an outcome of the earlier phases, based on the worker's growing independence and the supervisor's help towards self-reliance. But officially there was to be an artificial end to the relationship – it was to be determined by time, September 1966. Most workers were not ready for this. They did not feel that they had acquired sufficient understanding and skill to work on their own. This produced anxiety which was turned into pressure on themselves and the supervisor in order to be competent in the allotted time. The supervisor realised it was impossible for ten people to reach the same stage at a given moment. She too felt pressured, and for two weeks did not understand what was happening. In this period tensions were evident, the learning slowed up, and instead of relieving the pressure the supervisor added to it.

A seminar which should have been about supervision was devoted to a discussion about the future. The problems were thrashed out. By this time the responsibility of the project was shared more fully by the whole group, and it was agreed that the artificial time limit should be discarded, that supervision should be used by workers as long as they required it, and that seminars should be more frequent. The thinking behind this was that the group setting should gradually replace the individual setting (supervision) for learning, but that the latter should be discarded by a worker only when he wanted to do so. When this decision was made, tensions were relieved and only one or two needed time to accept their awareness that they were unable to 'qualify' at a given date. With the relief of tensions, the new phase in the relationship was understood, and this helped other learning to continue. At the time of writing this report, workers are moving at their individual pace to a stage when only infrequent consultations are required.

The conclusions of this chapter might well be that a relationship cannot be taken for granted – that its potential cannot be fully realised until the participants understand and accept its nature, and the factors within it. But when they do understand, they are able to work more effectively, within a relaxed atmosphere, to achieve the purpose of the relationship. It was hoped in the project, that the experience of the supervisory relationship, as well as their understanding of it and their learning within it, would contribute to the workers' understanding when they accepted responsibility for a similar relationship with new leaders.

CHAPTER FIVE

Material for Sessions

THE supervisory sessions consisted of discussions about the worker in his job. The workers understood that they were responsible for presenting the material, and for deciding what it would be about. In this chapter we are concerned with the subjects presented, patterns in their presentation, and some of the reasons why particular subjects and patterns emerged. The use of material is considered only in relation to this.

SUBJECTS PRESENTED

The range of subjects was almost as wide as the number of factors in youth work permitted, but they could be divided into three main areas, the situation, the worker's role and behaviour, and the worker himself. For the purpose of clarity in this chapter, the word 'area' is used to describe these three main headings, and the word 'subject' is used to describe any topic which comes within any of the three areas.

The situation included:

1. Membership (and other young people) – individual and group behaviour, expectations, attitudes, values, ages, activities, relationships, needs, development, etc.
2. Volunteers and staff – behaviour, expectations, attitudes, values, relationships, roles, skills, status, training, etc.
3. Management committee – behaviour, expectations, attitudes, values, relationships, function, authority, policy, etc.
4. Youth officer and/or other officials – behaviour, expectations, attitudes, values, functions, relationships, authority, policy, etc.
5. Neighbours and parents – behaviour, expectations, attitudes, values, involvement, etc.
6. Other youth workers and officials from schools and social agencies – behaviour, expectations, attitudes, values, involvement, service, etc.
7. The numerous ways in which these individuals and groups related to each other.

The worker's role and behaviour included:
1. The behaviour expected of him within the situation

2. All aspects of his behaviour with individuals and/or groups and in relating individuals and groups to each other (including administrative work).

The worker himself included:

his knowledge, thinking, feeling, understanding and skill, which affected his role and behaviour, and therefore the situation too.

It is obvious that the three areas were rarely completely isolated. If the subject were the management committee (the situation), the worker's role or attitude was frequently included. If a worker talked about his role, it was usually in relation to some individual or group in the situation. If he talked about his ideas or feelings, he was normally relating these to his role and/or some part of the situation. The areas were therefore normally discussed in relation to each other.

It was important, however, that the areas should be identified for two reasons.

First, it was necessary for both worker and supervisor to understand the angle from which the material was being presented. If a worker said, 'I am worried about Jim's group', and went on to describe the behaviour of Jim's group and how he had dealt with it, the worker was bringing in his feelings, his behaviour, and several subjects relating to membership. Possibly all three had to be explored, but depending on previous sessions, on the worker's needs, knowledge and awareness, and the supervisor's understanding of these, a decision had to be made as to where the problem lay or where learning was important – in understanding young people and group behaviour, in understanding the worker's role, in considering why the worker was worried, or in relating all three. Identification and clarification were therefore essential from the beginning.

Second, it was useful to identify the areas in order to understand the different ways in which they were sometimes presented in relation to each other. F described a group incident in which group members had damaged the club. She said she was worried, not because of the members, but because of what the adults might think. She did not stop at describing the adults' attitude, but continued with the structure of the club, and the functions, powers and communication of the adults within it. Finally, she talked about her own role in this. Her presentation of areas one after another led her eventually to the one she was most concerned about at that time. A started by saying, 'I felt superfluous at the club'. In order to work out the reason, he described what he did (behaviour), what was happening in the club (situation), and his own understanding

37

of youth work (self). He presented the subject – his feeling, and then branched out into three directions in order to find the solution.

In these two examples the workers moved from one area to another in different ways and for different reasons. It was useful to identify the areas, therefore, not only in order to discover the problem area or the learning point, but in order to establish how the three areas – the situation, the worker's role and behaviour, and the worker himself– were or could be related to each other.

Obviously, the subjects too could be separated in many different ways for presentation and consideration. Adults could be separated from young people, administrative work from work directly with people, the situation inside the club from the situation outside, work with individuals from work with groups. Subjects were constantly being isolated in order to study them and then relate them in a new way.

G spent several sessions studying the behaviour of membership groups. A problem then arose concerning his management committee. G said, laughing at himself as he did so, 'I could cope with the club very well without the committee'. The management committee problem was then considered, and led to a discussion about the expectations, attitudes, and participation of the management committee members, and the purpose and function of the committee. G's role within the committee was discussed next, and finally the similarities and differences between the committee and a membership group, and how the two related within the club. In this way the subject of the management committee (seen as a burden) was isolated, explored, and then brought back into the situation (as an integral part). With such a vast amount of relevant material, it was necessary through time for both worker and supervisor to understand the importance of isolating a subject for exploration, but only as a temporary measure before relating it to others for greater understanding and efficiency.

THE FIRST PATTERN IN PRESENTING MATERIAL

The pattern common to all workers in the earlier sessions was that several subjects were presented each time – sometimes separately and sometimes as one subject leading from another. Normally this pattern lasted for two, three or four sessions, but in two instances it covered nine sessions. In the first session most workers gave a picture of their total situations, described from different angles, such as, 'This is the situation in which I am working', 'I am having a difficult time because this is the situation in which I am working,' or 'The work is both interesting and problematical. This is the situation.' In the following sessions, the description of some of the subjects was repeated, sometimes with a different emphasis or with the inclusion of new factors.

This pattern of presentation appeared to have several possible sources. At first a worker wanted to give the supervisor a picture of the setting from which all future discussion would develop. Some workers were considering the subjects which seemed appropriate for supervision. Some wanted to know which the supervisor would want, and would follow her lead in developing any one of the subjects, or after presenting several, would say, 'This is what I'd like to discuss. Is it relevant?' Other workers had not decided on the areas in which they wanted help, and ranged over several subjects, either hoping the supervisor would help them discover this, or that they would find out for themselves as they continued to talk. Sometimes a worker waited to see what was likely to happen in the sessions before presenting a subject on which he wanted help. Sometimes one preferred to present several 'happy' situations before presenting a problem. Some workers felt so inundated with problems that they presented several in one session.

When this first pattern lasted for a longer period, it was sometimes because a worker wanted to use the supervisor as a sounding board for his own ideas and opinions. He wanted an intellectual discussion, and to make judgements about what was happening, rather than examine the situation. If the supervisor tried to help him look at a situation, he tended to change the subject.

Three examples of the first pattern:

EXAMPLE I

SESSION I

F started by presenting, as a problem, the behaviour of a group in the club one evening. Discussion led to her expression of concern about the adults' attitudes and expectations of the club. She then described all the adults connected with the club, and the lines of communication between them, and then her own role. Finally she returned to the behaviour of the group already described and explored her own attitudes to it.

SESSION 2

F presented a second problem – a group had broken into the club. Her handling of the situation was discussed. She then described as separate subjects, the management committee, the volunteers, and her own feelings and worries.

SESSION 3

F presented as a problem the behaviour of two girls. She described her own behaviour in relation to them. F then talked about individual members of the management committee, and finally, her own role in the club.

SESSION 4
F described the problems of the management committee and her own role within it.

Comments
F would say that at first she thought supervision was about problems so she started with one. But there were two other factors. First F had not worked out clearly where her problems lay, and secondly she also thought supervision related only to membership groups. So in each session F started by discussing a problem, a membership problem. She was unable to prevent herself from talking about adults, and her relation to them – which at the time was her main concern. After three sessions she realised this was acceptable in supervision and concentrated on it.

EXAMPLE 2

H spent the first four sessions describing his club, his work in it, its problems, and his concern about it. He did this in great detail, and included organisational structure, the place of the club within it, his relations with adults, the other clubs in the neighbourhood, the problems of violence, drugs, lack of activities, and his own role with the members. In each session all subjects were presented in a complete circle, the circles getting smaller each time, and with a different emphasis. In the first two sessions it seemed evident that H was feeling overburdened by the multi-racial and violent aspects of the club, and was feeling unsupported. He seemed to be manoevering effectively among the different groupings, but he felt that although members seemed to appreciate him and the club, he was on a volcano which might erupt. H then emphasised his own role and reasons why members came to the club. He thought that his difficulty might be in not being able to explain the positive things that were happening in the club, and in his feeling inadequate because he could not help the members to do more. In the following session H brought records of group behaviour in order to explore what he and the members were doing, so that he could learn to explain it in different ways.

Comments
H did not know where he wanted help in his work, and continued to cover a wide range of subjects until this emerged through mutual agreement. He saw supervision as a situation in which he could get help in identifying areas in which he wanted help, and continued to supply as much information as possible until this happened. He also saw it as a situation in which he could unburden himself, another reason for covering this wide range. This method of presentation linked up with one point at which H later decided that he wanted help – in explaining what he was doing. He could describe situations very vividly in narrative form, but found it difficult to analyse them, draw conclusions, and explain what he was doing as a result.

EXAMPLE 3

J described his total club situation in his first session, and then for four sessions concentrated on a group – the same group for two sessions, and different groups for the third and fourth. In his fifth session J covered a wide range of subjects related to problems in changing jobs. This continued for the next three sessions.

Comments

J saw supervision as a situation in which he could learn about groups. He did not want to present problems unless they were about membership groups. But his change of work presented numerous problems, and being unable to concentrate on a group, he presented the problems. When these were accepted and discussed J had to reconsider what he most wanted to learn about in supervision and this took time.

It can be seen that although there was a similarity in pattern, in that workers presented several subjects in the earlier sessions, the ways in which they were presented were completely different for each worker, depending on his feelings, his expectations, and his understanding of his own work. This was a period of exploration, and in order to help a worker, the supervisor had not only to think about the material presented, but to try to understand the reasons behind the particular pattern of presentation.

A SECOND PATTERN

A new pattern emerged after a few sessions, in that a worker presented only one subject, or at the most two, in one session. Occasionally he would revert to several subjects either because he thought they could be covered satisfactorily in one session, or because several subjects weighed heavily upon him.

Continuation of three examples:

F SESSION   4 Management committee.
               5 Management committee.
               6 Inter-group behaviour.
               7 Management committee.
                 A difficult group. Plans for a volunteers' meeting.
               8 Evaluation.
               9 Volunteers' meeting.
               10 A group incident.
               11 Conflicts in club policy.
               12 Conflicts in club policy.

41

H SESSION	6 Record of groups.
	7 Record of groups.
	8 Annual report. Staff relationships.
	9 Evaluation.
	10 Record of groups.
	11 Record of group
	12 Record of groups.
	13 Club policy.

J SESSION	10 Camp. Plans for volunteers' meeting.
	11 Volunteers' meeting.
	12 Worker's role in the club.
	13 Camp. Winter plans. Recording.
	14 Volunteers.
	15 Members' group.
	16 Staff meeting.

Perhaps it should be noted again at this stage, that while concentration was now seen to be on one subject, it was not to the exclusion of others. The difference from the pattern of presenting several subjects, was that the other subjects were discussed only as they radiated from the main subject and were related to it. The last subject mentioned – the staff meeting – led to discussion on staff relationships, group behaviour, club structure, membership needs and worker's role, but only as they related to the staff meeting.

This second pattern showed a concentration on and exploration of one subject at a time - the subject on which a worker wanted help, or in which he wanted to learn more. But this pattern also pointed up a lack of continuity, for which there were several reasons.

The first was that sometimes a subject was explored to a worker's satisfaction in one session. The second and main reason was the complexity of the work, as can be seen at the beginning of this chapter. There were numerous aspects of his job which a worker wanted to understand more clearly, and frequently he presented the one he was thinking most about that week. Events and developments occurred with such rapidity that a worker's mind was constantly moving from one to another, and this was reflected in supervision. The third reason which was similar was the emergence of problems. Workers sometimes explored a group or situation and wanted to continue this the following session, but by that time there was an emergency or new problem and the worker needed to explore what had happened. It would have been unrealistic at such times in such a complex situation for supervision to be an added pressure; it was there, if required, to help sort out immediate problems as a part of ongoing learning. A fourth reason for the change of subjects related to recording, which will be discussed later in the chapter. If a worker wanted to learn to record his work, he sometimes produced a subject because it was possible to record it. The emphasis was therefore sometimes more on what could be recorded in order to learn about records, than on a situation about which a worker wanted to learn.

It is probable that most of these reasons applied to all workers at some point, although the strength of the reasons depended on the individual. Sometimes it depended on whether a worker could cope with his problems, or wanted to learn about a particular aspect, or whether he had previously held back difficulties, or wanted to concentrate on recording, or on how deeply he was prepared to explore a situation. But all reasons had one thing in common. They were now strongly related to the worker's need and/or his understanding of points at which he wanted to learn. In this second stage the worker was accepting responsibility not only for the presentation of material, but for the choice of appropriate material. The choice was discussed with the supervisor on occasions, but it was the worker who made the decision.

With such rapid changes, it was inevitable that the supervisor would wonder about the outcome of a situation discussed the previous week. She had to learn to go on wondering, for if she heard about this at all, it was usually two or three sessions later.

A THIRD PATTERN

The third pattern in presenting material was one in which continuity gradually developed. The average period from the beginning of the second pattern – single subjects – to a pattern of continuation, was fifteen sessions, although for one or two workers this lasted much longer. The continuity could be seen in two forms. The first was in relating subject to subject, session to session, and the second was in the development of one subject.

In the first form of continuity, some workers, having dealt with problem areas, concentrated longer on exploring some aspects of group behaviour from recorded material. Others spent more time in studying their own role in relation to all groups and individuals. The subjects might vary, but it became possible to transfer knowledge about one group, to understanding another type of group, or to compare knowledge of individuals in a group, to intergroup behaviour. The planning of a coffee bar could be related to administrative requirements and possibilities, and also to association among young people. The process was slow and it could not be said that all workers could relate all aspects of their work. But the emphasis in presentation became less on isolated subjects and more on relating subjects. This continuity came about sometimes because a worker was more aware of his job as one complex whole, sometimes because the supervisor was constantly relating factors, and often from a mutual, though frequently unspoken, understanding between the supervisor and worker that in order to be effective, a worker needed to understand bow subjects and areas related.

There were some events in the total setting which could be seen either as an interruption of the continuity or as an opportunity for relating more factors. Sometimes they were both. The club of one worker was burned down, and five workers changed jobs during the project period. In several instances the emotional upheaval created by the change was presented as a separate subject and considered. In all cases, the numerous factors in being deprived of a building or changing jobs had to be explored. In this sense the events could be seen as an interruption in the continuity. But when a job was changed during the later sessions, it was possible to relate all the subjects considered earlier, to the expectations, attitudes and plans in the new job. A new potential in relating factors or subjects could be explored. A new subject – the new job, was discussed, but in relation to the subjects explored earlier.

The second form of continuity, developing one subject, was usually the result of process recording. Three workers continued to explore members' behaviour and their own roles. One worker studied staff meetings, which were mainly training sessions. But the most significant continuity started when workers began to practise supervision. From that moment onwards, except for occasional moments of crisis, workers concentrated on one subject – supervision.

This in itself seemed in one sense like an interruption in continuity to the supervisor. She wondered if another few weeks or months would have made a difference to some workers in that they might understand groups more clearly, or see their jobs more completely as a whole. (Two workers continued for several months longer before supervising.) But within sessions workers had also been helped to understand some aspects of supervising, which was the overall continuity of the project. Seven (within three months of each other) were ready to practise supervision. They wanted to do so – this was their goal and their original reason for supervision. So their supervising became the next subject, and the continuing subject. In the event, it was through supervising that some workers learned to relate other factors.

It might be interesting to note that in the first pattern the worker was thinking more about the supervisor and himself, in understanding expectations and needs. in the second pattern, he was thinking more about his own needs and learning. In the third, he was thinking more about his own learning, together with the needs of the person he was supervising. None of these were exclusive of other factors, but the emphasis was obviously there.

A DIFFERENT KIND OF PATTERN – VERBAL OR RECORDED MATERIAL

Most of the workers thought they ought to present recorded material. Three reasons emerged. First they were part of a growing body of opinion that believed recording was the right thing to do. Secondly some believed that there was a correct way of recording, and they expected to be taught this in supervision. Thirdly some had found value in recording and wanted to develop their use of recorded material.

The supervisor believed that recording could be a valuable aid to learning, although she did not see it as essential at all times – this would depend on what workers needed. She accepted the workers' need to learn to record, but thought that as in other areas of learning in supervision, the learning should be from practice. The supervisor then made it clear that workers could choose to present their material verbally or in records. When given the choice, all workers presented their material verbally in the early sessions, and there appeared to be three types of reasons for this - practical, emotional, and the fact that it seemed inappropriate to record some subjects which were to be discussed.

The practical reasons were numerous. Without exception, the workers were very busy, working overtime most weeks, whether or not they were organised people. This in itself might not have affected recording, but most had no clerical help, and their typewriters were old. Several could not type. Fifty per cent of the recording was handwritten. To present a full recording could mean a morning's work, particularly when workers were not sure what to record. Added to this difficulty was the attitude of some colleagues or committee members who believed that records for training purposes were a waste of time. From a practical point of view therefore it could be a constant struggle to find time to record adequately in a slightly hostile atmosphere.

The emotional reasons varied. Some workers found it difficult to commit themselves to paper, particularly when it was to be shown to another person. At the beginning, when workers felt that they and their work would surely be judged by the supervisor, some felt that talking was safer. Others wanted to learn theoretically the 'right way' or the 'supervisor's way' of recording before trying it out. Concern about spelling and grammar, and difficulties in expressing themselves, prevented some from recording at first, or affected their attitude to it. For these reasons workers found recording difficult, although one might produce a record and ignore it, or say he wanted to record and not do so, or accept a suggestion that an incident might be recorded and not record it.

Even when accepting all these possible reasons for presenting verbal material instead of records, it still seemed that some situations and subjects could be more usefully discussed from verbal material. Particularly in the early days when workers wanted to describe the total situation, when they were trying to find out their own areas of difficulty or the points at which they wanted to learn more, records would have been an irritation – the field from which choices were to be made was too vast and too complicated. Later, when complicated communications between adults was a subject, or when a conflict developed. in which many groups and individuals were involved, or when a worker arrived feeling fed up with everything and not knowing why, records seemed inappropriate. A discussion might result in one area being isolated for recording later, but discussion seemed the priority. There were times too when a worker wanted to reflect on his learning, or to consider some aspect of his behaviour which he wanted to change, or the implications of changing his job. Records would have been superfluous on these occasions. It was essential, therefore, that workers and supervisor should understand where verbal or recorded material was the more appropriate, and then recognise some of the other reasons why a worker was not recording when he said he wanted to.

Although there were so many reasons for workers presenting verbal material, and although on occasions everyone did so throughout the project, in time every worker began to record fairly regularly. At some stage, each worker found a situation or group which he wanted to understand, or a problem he wanted to solve, and decided he would write about it. Obviously such a decision did not come automatically. It would dawn on the worker who wanted to know the 'right way' to record, that the supervisor wouldn't or couldn't tell him, so he could only find out by trying. Also, workers who were describing situations were pressed to produce more information, or evidence for opinions and judgements.

'They had a good evening' 'What made it good?'
'I can't get on with my chairman' 'Tell me about him'
'I know I did the right thing' 'What made it seem right?'
'The volunteers want me to tell them what to do' 'What in their behaviour makes you feel they want this?'

'The group had to be put out of the club' 'What was happening? What brought you to that decision?'

Workers found themselves constantly exploring their own statements, and were sometimes unable to provide factual evidence, or, when they considered more factors, realised that their original statement was not necessarily accurate. They could then see a practical value in recording, or that supervision couldn't be as helpful as it might because of a lack of factual material. So when a limited situation arose (e.g. group project, camp, or a conflict in a group) to which they could give the necessary time for observation, participation and recording, or in which they had real difficulties, workers linked this with their own need for factual information and began to record. The following three examples are of ways in which recorded material was introduced, together with the attitudes of workers and supervisor to it.

EXAMPLE 1

G preferred to discuss his work theoretically. He could absorb theory and discuss it very easily. This meant that he was more interested in knowing how to record than in recording. He had a very demanding job and no clerical help. In his interview and in his first session G explained that he had recorded in the past, but had not found the records particularly useful, and he felt there must be a correct way to record and wanted to learn it. This was discussed and S said she would help G to use records if he wrote them. In G's second session, he presented six sentences in abbreviated English about incidents in the club. S helped G to produce more information around the sentences, and G seemed surprised at some of the points which emerged. He then asked how helpful the records were. S asked G if he thought they had been helpful. G thought they had been, but that they needed more detail and he hadn't time. He said records were essential, and S asked for what purpose. G said he had been taught this in college but had not been able to discover their use as learning material. S suggested that from their discussions about recording, G seemed more concerned about recording properly than in understanding his work. Would it be an idea to forget about recording for a while until he knew what he wanted to record? G agreed and presented verbal material for the next three sessions, first several subjects at a time and finally only one subject, a group situation. In the following session G produced a tape-recording of a meeting he had led with the group, saying, 'Could we listen to this? I don't know what to look for in it, but I'd like to understand what is happening in the group.' G learned several things from the tape, and said he would listen again and make notes on extracts. For the next two sessions G produced verbal material about his work with groups, after which he started to post brief records in advance, and arrived at sessions knowing what he wanted to discuss from the records. Four sessions later G sent in several typed sheets or records describing a camp weekend.

47

These were used for three sessions, the records were explored each time, and G worked on questions and analysis between sessions. He continued to use recorded material in sessions, but on one occasion said he had started to record a management committee meeting but could not do so. He said, 'If there is a problem it is easy to record, but without one it is difficult to know how to start'. S and G then explored the meeting to find out what would be useful to know about it. Afterwards G prepared a series of questions for himself about the meeting. When G began to supervise he had periods when he did not record – again he found the slow method of learning frustrating. At the same time he became anxious about his skill in supervising. He was quickly able to link the, two, and realised that he became anxious when he was unable to look carefully at what had happened and understand it.

Comments

G found learning through looking at situations and studying them, slow and frustrating, and therefore although he wanted to know how to record, the process of observing, deciding what to write and then writing, was irritating. S felt that G needed help in learning from his experience, and she was not forthcoming theoretically. When G ignored recording for a while he was able to study his work, and this was a from stepping stone to seeing the point of recording. S was prepared to help G learn from any type of record he produced. The camp record was an opportunity for G to learn about his work and to learn for himself how to use a process recording. From this moment, G was able to relate the two, and although he still became frustrated at times with the slow speed, particularly when he wanted to supervise well, he understood both his frustrations and the value of recording. He had no difficulty in writing full records, producing material from which he could learn a great deal, when he saw the value, gave up the struggle to learn theoretically, and gave himself time.

EXAMPLE 2

D never mentioned recording in the early days but presented verbal material. He could describe members and group behaviour with understanding, and had absorbed much theory. A difficulty in some sessions was that he was liable to switch his position in a discussion if he felt it was untenable, but at first he seemed unaware of doing this. S thought records would be a help to D in overcoming this, though on reflection she must also have believed they would help her.

After four sessions on verbal material, S said in the fifth that if D could record some of the group behaviour it might be more helpful than theoretical discussion. D was non-committal. In the seventh session S said that records with examples might be more factual and help the discussion. D was non-committal. In an evaluation in the next session D gave examples of awareness about his own behaviour which he said had come from having to express himself on situations. He realised he needed to impress people and to defend his standpoint, and that this sometimes made him colour what had happened in an incident discussed. It was agreed that records might help D to avoid this. D then recorded briefly and factually regularly His grammar and spelling were not always easy to understand but if a comment were made it was only for clarification. In an evaluation a few months later, D said he had started to record because he knew S wanted him to – he could now see the value but couldn't yet describe it. He also said that his language difficulty had always worried him, but that it had been a help to discuss his writing without having his mistakes pointed out.

Shortly after this, D stopped recording, and for three months concentrated through verbal material on his situation, role and behaviour. Suddenly, and without discussion, D knew what he wanted to record, the questions he wanted to ask, and how he wanted to analyse his records. He evolved his own methods, without too much writing, to bring in a growing variety of facts, together with analysis.

Comments

D did not want to record. S was unable to help D to be factual in the early days. she saw records as helping in this. The records did help D to be factual and he learned a great deal about himself in his work through studying them. But in order to sort out more deeply, numerous aspects of his work, D abandoned recording material. When he understood these more clearly, he was able to see new values in recording. At the time S's attitude to records in D's learning seemed appropriate and he learned as a result, but the question remains as to whether continued discussion of verbal material instead would have been equally or more advantageous for D's training.

EXAMPLE 3

A wanted to learn about his work in any way possible. At first be was unaware of how much he knew, or could not acknowledge it. He lacked confidence not only in his ability to record, but in his understanding of his job.

In A's first two sessions, he presented verbal material. In his third he discussed the variety of groups in a club, and then asked about methods of recording. This was discussed and related to the earlier discussion of groups. S suggested that a sociogram might help A understand the relation between the groups. In the next session (and a later one) A produced a sociogram which was studied. Then A produced records of sessions with staff and a boy's group. The following week A said he had left his records behind and a problem was discussed. In the seventh session A said it was difficult to know what to record. Several problems were considered from which emerged A's worry about his own role in the club. S suggested that it might be useful to record what A did in the club – as many incidents as he could remember – so that his role might be clarified. The following session A brought a record of an expedition with a description of his own behaviour. He then continued to record regularly in different ways for different purposes. He sometimes expressed reservations about his ability to record, and his English, or the wish that S would say if he were recording well. But A was able to smile about this and it became less important as his own confidence in his work developed.

Comments

A wanted to record and did so regularly. He wanted the opinion of S about his records but she did not give it, as she felt he should judge the value for himself. She did, however, suggest methods or subjects for recording, because she believed A's need for confidence in what he was doing was more important than his need to take the initiative in making suggestions at that time. Most of A's learning throughout the project was from recorded material.

The pattern in recording material was closely related to the other patterns already described. Workers recorded different subjects for different sessions. Slowly, material from different records was related, and some workers started to record the same group, or groups, week by week. Just as the introduction of supervision practice brought workers to concentrate on one subject, so it brought those workers who were not already involved in process recording to becoming involved. With rare and temporary exceptions, all workers presented recorded material of their supervisory sessions regularly, and it was at this stage, perhaps belatedly, that some workers began to understand different ways of recording sessions, and to analyse, question and draw their own conclusions from their recorded material.

It might sound as though regularity in presenting recorded material was an achievement towards which everyone had worked. This is partially true, for workers wanted to record, and recording was seen as a valuable tool in learning. Also, workers were preparing to supervise, and the supervisees would arrive freshly trained from college – some would certainly bring recorded material, and would want help in using it. This was an added reason for workers to learn to record their work and to use the records. But alongside these incentives two factors were recognised. Workers had to overcome their desire to record because it was 'the thing to do', and learn to record and use recorded material because it was useful to them. In doing this the second factor emerged – that recording was not always possible, and that sometimes it was neither essential nor appropriate for their learning.

The content of supervision was therefore material presented by workers for discussion – material about their situations, their roles, and their behaviour as it affected these. Although there were individual reasons for patterns in presenting material, the patterns with modifications were common to all workers. Because the content was about their work, most workers covered similar subjects, but because of the nature of the work there was a great variety of subjects. But there was no plan and no programme to be covered. Each worker presented his own material for discussion for his own reasons, although at first he sometimes needed help in understanding his reasons, and in understanding what he most needed to learn. He learned from the material he presented, but the ways in which he was able to learn provides the material for the next chapter.

CHAPTER SIX

Learning-Ways and Means

THE whole point of supervision was that workers should learn, in order to help their understanding and effectiveness. They brought to supervision material from which to learn, and as they understood the supervisory relationship and its possibilities, so they were able to use it to help their learning. There were several ways in which workers could and did learn, although each one had his own particular approach. This chapter will explore some of the methods of learning, before describing the individual approaches which emerged in supervision.

In the youth work setting, many words constantly appear-observation, insight, understanding, intellect, feeling, theory, concept, intuition, knowledge, skill. In one sense, the variety of ways in which these words are used might well reflect a confusion in thinking about learning. In another sense, it appears to reflect an attempt to see learning as requiring the application of the total person. If this is so, some of the difficulties in learning, and in understanding learning, might arise from being unable to use all of oneself, or from being unable to see how different parts of learning relate. For this reason, an attempt is being made here to describe, by isolating aspects for consideration and then relating them to each other again, how the whole person might be used in learning.

LEARNING TO RELATE THEORIES AND PRACTICE

The youth worker's learning is mainly about people (including himself), together with as many factors as possible which affect people. When he begins his training he expects to acquire a theoretical and practical understanding and a new experience of people, so that he can become familiar with his and their nature and behaviour, and extend his range of information about them. He also wants to develop skill in understanding and working with them. He acquires this knowledge and skill in college and on the field.

Starting from theories
If a student or worker studies theories from books or lectures, he

becomes conscious of the new theories and can describe them. He uses his eyes and ears to take them in and his mind absorbs them. Perhaps he can describe several theories as to why two people in the same family are different, or why a group of adults behave differently from a group of children. But the theories are still a series of sentences which are repeated parrot-fashion. He might appear to accept them because he wants to qualify, because be likes the lecturer, because he wants to be in agreement with his fellow students, or because he is conditioned to agreeing with something presented in an authoritative way. But these are emotional reasons arising from his own needs. In order to grasp the theories and understand them, he has to draw out his own experience of families, children's groups and adult groups, and bring them to bear on the theories. He also needs new experiences of observing children and adults, so that he can apply these also to the theories.

If a student is told (with explanation) that all groups have leaders and sub-groups, the facts go into his mind and can remain there unused. But if he is asked to go into a club and look for leaders and sub-groups, he consciously sees and meets people in the club and works out in that situation what he thinks makes a leader in the group, or a sub-group among friends. He brings his mental experience of what he sees, to bear on the theory that leaders and sub-groups exist in a group. This coming together of the facts of theories from outside, and his thinking inside about his own observations, is the point at which the student begins to learn the theory – to perceive its meaning, and understand it.

When the student begins to perceive the meaning of the theory, the application of his experience might lead him to believe that it is valid for him. But wider experience of groups might make him think that all groups don't have sub-groups, that there are times when groups don't appear to have a leader. He now has a choice – to stop his thinking at the point where his experience no longer fits in with the theory (I must be wrong), to discard the theory and find other ways of describing his experience, or to apply his wider experience to the theory, to see how it might be modified, or how it relates to other theories. If he takes the last course, he is now adding his ideas, from his experience, to the theory – presumably the way in which many theories have evolved – and is learning to deal with the theory in a different way.

An example of this has already been described in this report. Workers were taught that recording was valuable in that it was a tool which could help them in understanding their work. This was a theory which had been proved in different situations. Until they practised recording, this was to the workers a theory with no meaning. Some accepted the fact of the theory but did not record, and, being unable to apply experience to it, were unable to perceive any meaning in the theory. Some, after practising, perceived the meaning of the theory. Wider experience of recording told some workers that the theory did not apply to all aspects of their situation. At this point, some stopped thinking about the theory, but continued to record whether it helped or not. Some discarded the theory, and found other ways of helping themselves. Others worked out where the theory applied and where it did not, and were then able to add their thinking, from their own experience, to the theory.

Starting from practice

When a worker observes a group, he takes in the observations through his senses, to his mind. Here they could rest unused, without thought. But if the worker thinks about them, bringing his ideas to bear on them, he perceives meaning in what he observes. If he also understands a theory, he has a new range of information to use in thinking about the observations, and he also has a new language. A leader observes a group of eight members, and he hears John suggest dancing, and they all dance. Later he hears Nick suggest that they should go for a drink, and two follow him. John and the others stay behind. John starts a fight with another boy. The others ignore this and play records. The worker observes John, Nick, friends, dancing, fight, records. But he understands the theory that a group has leaders and sub-groups, so in his thinking he now sees John and Nick as leaders at different moments, how they relate to followers, and the ways in which the group divides into sub-groups. He understands his experience in terms of the theory, and so the experience has new meaning for him. At this moment his understanding might not make much difference to his action, but his theory has given him wider terms of reference from which to ask his questions, and make his decisions as to how he will work. At the same time he describes the situation in a different language, and whereas the theory without experience was merely a form of words, now it can be a clearer explanation of what he observes and what he is doing.

There are therefore four points at which the worker is learning about theories and experience through relating the two – once he has absorbed theoretical facts and observations of people. He perceives the meaning of a theory by bringing his personal experience to bear on it. He learns how to use and think about his experience so that he can understand how the theory can be dealt with – accepted, or modified.

He perceives a new meaning in his experience by reflecting a theory on to it. He learns how a theory can be used to improve his practice and provide him with new concepts from which to describe his practice.

LEARNING TO USE FEELINGS

The mind is defined as the seat of consciousness, thought, volition, and emotion. The last section was about learning through the use of thought – an intellectual learning – the theories and the experience were described in terms of logical connections of ideas. A worker saw something, he related it to other ideas and thought about it. But this section starts from feelings, which affect and are affected by ideas, and the connections between them.

The first point of learning through feelings for some workers, is in the recognition that they have feelings, and if they are unaware of them, in bringing them into the mind so that they are aware of them. There are emotional reasons why a worker tries not to accept that he feels sympathy, tenderness, compassion, anger, or fear. He might believe that his image should be that of a calm, controlled person, or that he might hurt people if he expresses his feelings, or his earlier experiences might have taught him that feelings should be hidden. So he denies his feelings and puts them out of his mind. But even though they are hidden, they are liable to affect his conscious behaviour. For example, a worker who feels fear that he will not be able to control his club, might spend his time working out how he can impose and enforce discipline, and prevent trouble. He might give as reasons that a worker should be respected, or that young people should care for property, or need a firm authority. He might be unaware that his fear exists, and lf he is satisfied with the results of his actions, might never understand that fear is one of the motives behind them. If he is not satisfied, he might feel frustrated – baffled, defeated – and unless he can learn to recognise that his feelings have helped to create the problem, it is unlikely that he will be able to solve it. His learning point here is in mental exploration of the factors in the club situation, including how he feels about it. He might then recognise that he is afraid.

But in order to perceive the meaning of this feeling, he needs to think about it in relation to his situation – the experience. He might find that he is afraid of what the management committee will say about his work, that he will lose his job, that the club will be burned down, or of what the members will do to him. It could be that his fear relates to earlier experiences. He might consider what his behaviour, based on the unacknowledged fear, is doing in relation to the needs of the young people. Once he sees the fear in concrete terms he perceives its meaning, how it is affected by his situation, and how it affects the situation.

It might be interesting to note a project experience. Several workers recognised that some of their behaviour was based on fear. When asked what was the worst that could happen in their situation, the main answers were, 'The club could be wrecked', or 'I could lose my job'. So they faced these things. It was no less a surprise when later one club was completely burned down (by an outsider), and two workers lost their jobs (not from inefficiency), but by that time these events were not seen as their worst fears being realised, but as situations to be dealt with.

Even so, in perceiving the meaning of feelings, through thinking about them in relation to the experience, a worker understands the feelings only in part. He can express them, and see what they do, but he has yet to learn how to deal with them and this can take a long time. For example, if a worker sees John and Nick breaking up equipment, and feels angry but denies this and is therefore unaware of it, he is liable in a calm way to stop them. But John and Nick might see a tight-lipped, white-faced person bearing down upon them, and whatever words are used, they are likely to see the anger. If this is what they want, the behaviour might be repeated. If the worker examines this situation and accepts that he is angry, for a while he might express his anger to John and Nick. It might have favourable results if John and Nick can understand relationships only in terms of feeling. But indiscriminate use of anger will not help each time. When he understands this, the worker wants to learn how to deal with his anger. He explores each situation in which he is angry, recognises its futility in terms of meeting members' needs, decides not to be angry next time, and he is. But each time he explores the situation, the range of information (which helps him understand it) about himself, other people and the situation, is increasing. His terms of reference are expanding. At some moment, sometimes difficult to explain, he is so much in tune with the members' needs that his own are not important to him, and he suddenly knows that he feels angry but doesn't have to express it. This learning point, which might seem more of a process than other learning points, is the one in which the worker understands his feelings, that is, he not only recognises they exist, and perceives their meaning, but knows how to deal with them, through applying his experience and his thinking to them.

In the last example, the worker learned to understand his feelings, through applying his thoughts to them – his thinking about himself, other people, and the situation in which they met. The feelings described could be seen as negative feelings in that they were were a denial of what the worker wanted to be. But other feelings are seen as positive in that workers want to use them, and see them as constructive. Some workers, for reasons mentioned earlier, want to deny those feelings too, in which case their learning about them is similar to learning about anger or fear. Others use them, and are aware of using them, but at an emotional level. They don't necessarily think about them. The learning points about these feelings are the same, but the use of them without thought needs to be explored.

A worker who consciously uses his feelings without applying reasoning to them could be called intuitive. He has an immediate understanding of something through his senses. This can happen when a worker senses an atmosphere in the club – he feels that something is building up, but he doesn't know what it is. He might take action based purely on these feelings – close the club early, create a diversion, or observe the trouble-makers more closely. Reflecting on it later, he might think that he sensed the atmosphere because of strange silences, the way people spoke to each other, or the way they glanced at each other. But if he had waited to apply reasoning to his feelings, he would have been too late.

It is because they have experienced feelings themselves that some workers understand how other people are feeling. They understand with their senses what it means to feel happy, fearful, depressed, pressured, to feel like behaving wildly, co-operatively, anti-socially, or to feel a sense of achievement, frustration and exhilaration. Such a worker feels sympathy or compassion because he is in tune to other people's feelings. The wider the range of his own feelings, and the wider the range of situations in which he has experienced these feelings, the greater his ability to understand feelings in other people, and possibly the greater his warmth towards them.

When using his feelings, the worker's learning is first in recognising that his ability to feel can lead him in two directions – in feeling *for* a person or in feeling *with* him – and in understanding how to change from the first to the second. One worker feels *for* a boy in trouble, *for* boys tearing round the room, or *for* a group which planned a dance that was not successful. He is remembering what he felt like when he was in trouble, when he felt like going mad, or experienced failure, and so he expects the boys and the groups, to have these same feelings. He is not thinking about the people outside himself, but is relating his observations of them to his own feelings and his own experience, and so he transfers his own feelings to them – feels *for* them. Another worker feels sympathy *with* the boys and *with* the group. Being able to feel, he also recognises that the boy has particular problems, that the boys have been working all day, or are reacting to various incidents in the club, that the group has put a great deal of work into the dance, and does not understand what went wrong, and looks miserable. He is relating his observations to known facts about the people outside himself, and to his feelings – the outcome is sympathy.

Although the first worker's feelings might well be similar to those of the boys or group, dependence on his feelings and his personal experience can lead to hit-or-miss judgements, as they and their situations are different from his. He might expect the boy in trouble to feel contrite, when in reality the boy feels angry and resentful, or he might feel that the boys feel lively and energetic, when they are feeling angry about his leadership. His learning, therefore, is in recognising the unreliability of his own feelings, and in concentrating his thinking on his observations of the other people concerned – on what he knows about them and the situation they are in, or the questions he might ask about it. In this way the first worker begins to bring his thinking to bear on his feelings, so that they can be used more effectively – in other words, to be the second worker.

Both workers are now in the same situation as the worker who was learning to deal with his anger. They are aware of their feelings and have understood their meaning. Their next learning is the same as his, in that they want to understand the effect of their sympathy on their actions. Again, an exploration of each incident is indicated so that the actions are understood in terms of how far they have met the needs of the members.

The worker's learning with negative and positive feelings is therefore not in how to repress them, but in becoming aware of them, in understanding how they can and do affect his work, and in relating to them his thinking about people and situations outside himself, so that he can use his feelings more effectively. In doing this a worker is no longer limiting himself to using only a part of himself but is bringing his intellect and feeling together, towards a more fruitful use of both.

LEARNING TO USE VALUES

Every worker has values which affect the work he is doing. They could relate to his religious beliefs, his professional training, and/or the variety of his experiences which have led him to think about, or accept without thinking, an approach to his own behaviour and that of other people. Some of these values are basic – basic to his ideas of himself and other people. This chapter is not a suggestion that a worker should change such values, but rather that he should recognise and understand them, and be open to change according to his increasing understanding of himself and other people.

Sometimes, however, a worker does not know what some of his values are, or how they are affecting his work, so it would seem that his first learning point is in bringing them into his mind – becoming aware of them. Values are sometimes carefully hidden. A worker talks of the importance of association for young people, but his face becomes animated when talking about members joining in a 'constructive' activity. He talks of the importance of the individual, but works towards getting members to conform. He talks of equal opportunities for boys and girls, but assumes that the chairman of the club is always a boy. Whatever the reasons for his behaviour, such a worker is not clear about what he believes, or is trying to accept two sets of values at the same time – one for the public, and one for himself. In other words, he is paying lip-service to one set of values, but his actions indicate his real values.

The worker's learning here is in bringing out into the open that he is saying one thing and acting another. He learns this through questioning or being questioned on his actions. What makes the activity 'constructive'? Is it the opposite of destructive? What is constructive about this activity which makes it different from other activities? These, and other questions leading from them, can help a worker to understand the source and meaning of his own judgements. At the same time, by applying his observations of people to his own statements, he learns the meaning of the statements in the same way as he learned the meaning of theories, after which he can decide for himself whether this is something he really believes in.

When values are explored in this way, an important learning is in understanding where they come from. A group of workers discussed gambling. Instead of continuing an argument they decided to consider where each worker's attitude had come from. One based his disapproval on his religious belief, though he had a difficult time working out how it related. Another had seen the effect of compulsive gambling. A third decided she didn't really disapprove but accepted a general and official opinion that it was wrong. They then looked at reasons why people gambled, its effect on young people, some of the harmful and helpful things young people could learn from gambling, and gambling in relation to other activities. No one appeared to change attitudes in the meeting, but some months later two workers commented on its effect on them. Both said that when boys had begun to gamble in the club, they had felt completely relaxed about it. There were no battles, but the workers observed what happened. In one case it faded out, and in the other, the group members gambled when they had nothing to do, and the worker accepted this. From this example, it would seem that just as the understanding of a feeling can affect a worker's actions in a club, so the understanding of his values and beliefs can take away an unrecognised pressure, and help him to behave in a more relaxed way.

Perhaps the most significant learning about values is in changing from accepting a set of rules – rights and wrongs – to judging behaviour in terms of a situation. Frequently, the worker's difficulty is not that he believes strongly in a particular set of rules, but that he is trying to find a blueprint for his behaviour in his work. He struggles to find an outside authority which will tell him what is right or wrong, or tries to convince other people that certain values are right or wrong. This leads to group discussions as to whether a worker should be permissive, or lead by example, whether workers should be called by christian names, whether clubs should be activity centred. One set of values is being put against another, and while this might be useful learning in terms of understanding that there are different points of view, it might still provide him only with a set of values to impose upon his work and the people in it. His alternative, if he wants one, is in learning how to relate his values to a situation.

Frequently workers understand that their behaviour seems inconsistent. A worker knows that he will reason with one boy and put another out of the club for the same behaviour. He knows that whereas this is sometimes the result of his mood of the moment, more often it is an understanding of the differing needs of the boys. His actions are a result of applying his understanding of the needs of the boys to his ideas of right and wrong. He has asked himself questions about the boys. In other situations, too, his understanding of actions in relation to his values can come only from constant questioning. Why am I bearing down on this card-playing group in anger? Is it because a management committee member might come in? Is the rule important? What is happening to the boys? What will be the result of this anger? Or, why am I insisting that they stay outside if they do not pay their shillings? Do I think it develops their characters? Is it because we need the money? How do they see money in relation to the club, or to me? Through such questions a worker begins to understand not only where his ideas of right and wrong come from, but other people's ideas of right and wrong and where they come from, and also other people's attitudes to his own values.

One worker described an incident in his club. At 9.30 p.m. he had asked a voluntary helper to get a group to put some equipment away. When he looked in a few minutes later, the boys were teasing the helper, and throwing the equipment to each other. The worker had stepped in, told the boys to put the equipment away, watched them do so, and then left the room. The worker said, 'At the time I thought I was right. Now I am not sure.' With questioning he explained that he had thought he was right because he wanted the equipment put away, and as the voluntary helper was not able to deal with it, it was his job to do so. His uncertainty came later when he wondered if he had been authoritarian. The worker was unconcerned about the helper and the boys, but only troubled about his own role and whether his behaviour was good or bad. He needed help in learning to judge his behaviour in the light of the situation he was in.

The worker then had to think – first about the boys, what did he know about them, what might have been expected of them in the light of this knowledge, reasons why they might be teasing the helper, how they reacted to and felt about the worker's behaviour; second, about the helper, how he felt about the job, whether he was at ease with the boys or afraid of them, how he saw his relationship with the boys, how he reacted to the worker's behaviour, and what he felt about it, the effect of the worker's behaviour on the helper's relationship with the boys; third, about the worker himself, his relationship with the helper and his expectations of it, how he wanted the boys to relate to the helper, and how he wanted the boys to see the staff in relation to each other; fourth, about the urgency of the situation – the need for the equipment to be put away, the time factor, and the worker's role and how he understood it. The worker then needed to consider his action in the light of all this information, in terms of its helpfulness to the boys, the helper, and himself.

In examining all these factors, separately and then together, the worker was analysing the situation, so that he could judge his behaviour, not in isolation, but as it affected everyone concerned. No longer was it a question of an overall right or wrong, but of what was the most helpful thing to do in that situation. The worker was taking into account the values of the helper and the boys and himself, and, in understanding all their attitudes and expectations, was able to apply his own values to the total situation, instead of to a set of rules.

This could seem a small incident to examine so minutely, but it had three learning points for the worker. First, he recognised the wide variety of factors that could be observed, related to each other, and understood, in order to take the most helpful action. Second, he perceived a meaning in the statement, 'you should accept that other people have values too', and knew how to deal with it. Third, he perceived a new meaning in his own values, and where they might come from. Such learning is a slow process of examining many incidents, but it would appear to be a way of resolving the conflict of rights and wrongs. At times, a worker might feel blown by the wind, but as he learns to explore total situations of which he and his values are a part, he finds that he becomes more confident in using the results of the exploration as a basis for his judgement, instead of searching for an outside authority.

LEARNING FROM THE SITUATION

In the first part of this section different aspects of learning were considered – first, an awareness of theories, feelings and values, and of that which is being observed; second, an exploration of theories, feelings and values, and of observations; and finally, bringing reasoning to bear on the theories, feelings and values in relation to observations. The purpose of this learning was to perceive the meaning of each of these aspects, and to understand how they could be used in relation to each other, so that the worker could understand them and be more effective in his work. Obviously, much of this learning takes place within the worker's situation – it is about himself in his work. But even so, his ability to learn from his work depends on the emphasis he gives to those things which are inside himself – theories, values and feelings, together with knowledge from his previous experience – and the emphasis he gives to these things which are outside himself – people in relationship to his work setting, of whom he is one.

When a worker moves into a job, he may or may not be aware of the theories, values, feelings, and knowledge which he has got, and he may or may not have skill in using them. But these he brings to the situation. He also brings an ability to observe, feel and think. His ability to learn from his situation depends on which of these is the more important to him – that which is inside him, or his ability to see, hear, feel and think about that which is outside him. The worker is expected to be in control of his situation. Either he sees his control in terms of imposing himself upon it, or in observing it and thinking of his observations in the light of his theories, values, feelings and knowledge. He has a choice between imposing himself upon – or understanding – his situation.

In the following three examples, a worker imposes himself upon his club. First, one worker has theories. He knows theoretically the value of self-determination, so decides that members will determine what happens in the club. Or he knows that a useful way for youth leaders to work is through the natural leaders in the club, so he looks for these leaders. Or he knows that young people like adventurous things to do, so he looks for some. Or he knows that the management committee expects him to be able to work with, and understand, young people, so he must live up to these expectations. He tries to make the situation fit in with his theories, and his first frustrations appear when some parts do, and some don't.

Second, one worker has experience and ideas from other situations. Perhaps in another club, members joined in certain activities, enjoyed them and had a sense of achievement, so he introduces them in this club. He has seen a group in another club become more responsible as a result of decorating a coffee bar, so he thinks it would be a good idea to get his own group to do the same. Ted had started a members' committee in his club and it was successful, so he tries it too. This approach could be that of Epaminondas going to market – he found that eggs smashed in his pocket, and his mother said to put them in his cap next time, but the next time he had to buy butter, and it melted on his head. For the worker, the approach might not end in such disaster, but he is liable to become frustrated if he depends on his ideas and they don't work.

Third, if the worker imposes his own values and feelings on the situation, he is liable to make judgements on superficial observations. He then gives opinions on the situations and believes his opinion to be fact. 'It was a good evening' (no trouble). 'The committee's difficult' (it didn't accept my idea). 'The helpers don't like having a new worker' (they said the members would object to paying every night). The worker believes these things to be true because this is how he feels in relation to his ideas of right and wrong, good or bad, but such belief in his snap judgements is leading to more frustrations.

If such a worker is not aware of what he is doing, he is liable to continue to impose himself on the club, and become increasingly frustrated when the results do not come up to his expectations. But if he is aware of what he is doing when he imposes himself in these three ways, he is on the way to learning from the situation, because he has started by understanding aspects of his own behaviour, and he is a part of the situation. So he can ask himself why this theory didn't work, what made the group accept this idea, what made him feel this way about the volunteers. He is able to start with a recognition, and/or an understanding of his own behaviour, and move from there to observations of things outside himself – how people react to his behaviour, and what is happening to them as a result of it.

Two aspects of learning from the situation

Although most workers have a sense of urgency in a new job, and have pressures which affect their approach to it, those who see control in terms of understanding the work are liable to learn from it in a more relaxed way, and take more time to observe and think about their observations. Such a worker is in the same position as the supervisor, who in order to help a worker effectively has to learn from him. His learning has two main aspects – active observation while with people, and active thinking and analysis when withdrawn from them.

In the first aspect of learning from the situation, through observation, the worker is not waiting or absorbing passively. He is merely using himself differently from the worker who imposes himself – he is hearing more than talking, watching more than demonstrating, drawing out more than imposing, participating more than organising. Instead of saying, 'I must be respected by the members', he is learning what kinds of behaviour a member respects. Instead of saying, 'I must put the club on the map', he is learning to read the map, and instead of saying, 'I must be non-judgemental' he is learning where he judges, for what reasons, and how other people feel themselves to be judged. Such active observation with all his senses calls for close contact with the people concerned. The more remote the worker the more limited the area of his learning and the more he theorises, but as he participates and opens all his senses, so he is able to understand feelings, values and needs. He also learns what people expect of him – how they see his role. Frequently this is the hardest part of a worker's learning, because normally he finds a variety of expectations from different groups and individuals. But it is only in seeing, hearing, and feeling them that he is able to recognise them, and move on to a second stage of learning, how to deal with them.

The second aspect of a worker's learning is thinking about his observations, so that their meaning is understood. A worker might hear a boy say very strongly, 'There isn't a God', and he might simply accept it as having been said, ignoring it or arguing about it. Or he might think about the observation, and ask himself what the boy meant – did he want to test out his opinion against others, was this a way of attracting attention to himself, was he feeling that nobody cared about him? In trying to understand the meaning of the observation, the worker is learning something about the boy. In a wider context the worker might observe a clash of opinions in the management committee as to whether the club should allow some of the anti-social members in, or restrict membership to those who are ready to co-operate. The worker might accept the clash as inevitable, or as annoying that there should be questions about it. Or he might ask himself – what are their values, what are they worried about, who is agreeing with whom, is this a clash of personalities or a clash of opinions? As the worker finds meaning in his observations, he learns about the committee members and the problem. Thinking about these observations requires questioning. The questions are about what he sees, hears, and feels outside himself, and he is able to find the questions from the knowledge inside himself. It is the only range of information which he has from which to ask his questions.

Just as a worker can limit the range of his observations by removing himself from close contacts, he can also limit his thinking and therefore his conclusions and actions by using only a proportion of his knowledge. Sometimes this could be because a worker has limited theoretical knowledge – perhaps, for example, he doesn't understand some of the implications of individual or group behaviour. Sometimes a worker has emotional reasons for not using himself as a factor in his observations. Sometimes he might not understand that his work is related to the community in which it exists. So in examining an incident, he cannot apply questions about group behaviour, or cannot examine his own behaviour, or cannot consider the effect of the community on the incident itself. This is where he needs outside help in order to extend his range of information.

If a worker doesn't know for himself that relationships between people affect the decisions they make, an outsider (which could be a supervisor) might ask of an incident, 'How did they behave towards each other ?' 'Do they like each other?' 'Could it be that the teacher doesn't like to disagree with the headmaster?' Or if the worker doesn't know that his feelings have affected his behaviour in an incident, an outsider might ask, 'How did you feel about it?' 'What did you hope from it?' The only purpose of the outsider is to extend the range of information from which the questions might be asked – sometimes it could be new information, but more frequently it could ring a bell in the worker's mind so that he remembers that 'relationships' or 'feelings' are factors to be considered.

The process of observing, thinking about, and questioning observations, applies equally to an incident with one boy as to the management committee, or the ongoing membership. But the more complex the setting, the wider the range of observations and information. This requires more thinking to be applied to relating the meaning of one set of observations to the meaning of another. The process, however, is always that of analysing, examining each observation minutely, then examining them in relation to each other, so that conclusions can be drawn as to what is happening and what should or could happen. Such learning helps the worker to change from giving a subjective opinion, to drawing considered conclusions, and being able to explain to other people what is happening.

The worker is learning to understand his situation then from two points; first from being in close proximity so that he can use all his senses to take in information about the members, and so that he can observe himself in relation to them; second, from withdrawing from the membership so that he can think about his observations in relation to each other and analyse the situation, and explain it. The worker is thus using himself in two capacities, as the learner and the analyser, and he is learning in both capacities. He is also acting in both settings – in the first he is acting according to his immediate understanding of the situation. In the second he is analysing the meaning of those actions in relation to the rest of the situation, drawing out conclusions from it and explaining it.

His learning in each setting is affecting his learning and action in the other. While in close proximity he is learning about himself and other people from observations, which he uses in his analysis. His analysis gives him new learning and new actions, so that he has more understanding with which to observe. Observations with more understanding then widen the range of information from which to question and analyse. Although a worker in close proximity has immediate insight about some situations – that is, he can penetrate into circumstances with understanding – his learning through examination and analysis enables him to gain new insights, so that an increasing amount of his immediate action is based on understanding of the situation, as opposed to snap judgements about it. At the same time his analysis of situations is providing him with new theories about it, so that he is not only learning to be more effective in his work, but is adding his own theories (which he can describe with understanding) to the body of knowledge about youth work.

Therefore an important aspect of the worker's learning from his situation, and normally one which happens from the beginning onwards, is in understanding that the learning is not for its own sake –

merely interesting to know. The worker is learning from the situation so that he can function more effectively among people, people in relation to each other, and so that he can add to the body of knowledge for other workers who want to do so. This is why the theories are of little purpose unless they are understood from the contact and warmth of people, and why thinking and analysing are abortive unless feelings are understood and become a part of them. The purpose of the learning, which might well seem a slow and time-consuming process, is not only more efficiency, but more efficiency and warmth. The worker becomes in control of his situation, not because he is the knowledgeable authority, but through his understanding of it. Problems, conflicts, strong feelings, frustrations, set ideas, judgements, activities, programmes, policies, and co-operation still exist, but the worker is able to recognise them, accept or change them, use them and describe them because he understands what they mean in terms of people in relation to each other.

If the staff in a meeting are arguing fiercely about the members and their activities, the worker who understands what is happening might see his role as waiting quietly until he can help the staff to reach some decision, either to refer the discussion or resolve it. The worker who does not understand it is liable to exert his authority over it, argue or opt out. In a club where members seem to be moving in all directions, where the noise is deafening, an outsider might be horrified. The worker who understands it might be having an exhausting time but he is merely keeping his mind and senses alert so that he can intercede anywhere at the appropriate moment. The worker who has had a tremendous row with his youth officer (or chairman or neighbour) knows that he need not have a sleepless night: he realises that he hadn't been able to explain clearly what he was trying to do in the club, that he had felt compelled to defend himself, that the youth officer was worried about his own responsibilities – and that there are areas where he can now take action to relieve the situation.

In all three cases, the worker, through understanding something about other people, his own role, and his own behaviour, is in control of the situation, when in an authoritative sense it would seem that he is not. His learning has been in becoming aware of what is happening through observing and thinking about his observations; in becoming aware of the meaning of what is happening through his exploration and analysis of observations; in understanding through relating the two, that which has to be accepted and that which can be changed, how he can accept and how he can change, and how he can explain it to other people.

LEARNING IN SUPERVISION

Supervision was seen simply as a setting in which workers were helped to learn from their situation. They started by describing their situation – the centre, the members, the community, their ideas about their jobs – and gradually sorted out the particular problems or subjects about which they wanted to learn. Sometimes the learning started with an examination of the factors surrounding a problem, in order to see where the problem lay, or to consider the steps that could be taken to solve it. Sometimes it started with an examination of a statement made, in order to make a distinction between fact and opinion, or to help a worker describe his work in his own language, in terms he fully understood. Later, learning continued through reflection – on incidents, or behaviour between people, or the role of the worker – when numerous factors could be examined, more could be drawn out and each related to the other so that situations could be more fully understood.

All the learning was from that which had happened, that which existed, which a worker had observed and which he felt needed clarification and thought. The more he explored his observations, the more fully he could understand them and draw considered conclusions from which to take action. Sometimes the exploration could be of an incident between two people. Sometimes it could be of the total structure of a centre. But always the process was the same, and its purpose was to find out how much was known about a situation, how much could be found out about it, and how fully it could be understood.

Supervision was the setting, the relationship, which was used to learn in this way. All aspects of his work, his role and his own behaviour as it affected these, were areas about which a worker could learn, and which he could explore. While a worker was using supervision to learn from his situation, he was also using all aspects of learning as described earlier in this chapter.

In exploring his situation, a worker was helped to become more aware of his own feelings, to understand how these affected his work, to accept and deal with positive and negative feelings, and in particular, to apply thought to his feelings.

The question of values arose frequently, and the main help needed was in understanding the different values within a setting and how these affected the work. Even when these were understood, it was difficult to accept and deal with them, because the variety was not only among the young people, but was among the adults who had responsibility for the

67

work. They had different ideas as to the purpose of the work, and of acceptable methods which could be used to achieve purposes. A worker sometimes required help in understanding his own values, in recognising his desire for a blueprint, in learning to judge his actions in terms of helpfulness to people at particular times, and in understanding and becoming confident in his own role. But he frequently needed help in explaining the values of one group to another group with other values, in recognising that which had to be accepted and that which could be changed, and occasionally in recognising when it was more helpful to remove himself from a conflict in values within which it was impossible for him to work.

At some stage most workers learned to perceive the meaning of theories by relating their experience to them, and to use theories to throw light on observations and provide new concepts from which to describe them. They were already relating some theories to practice and finding satisfaction in doing so, but all were frustrated at times because practice did not fit into theories, or because theories did not throw light on practice. But when workers learned from observing, and examining, exploring and analysing observations, so they began to theorise about a situation and relate one theory to another. Most workers had little time for reading; those who made time found a new interest in parts of text-books, or in comparing theories.

Although supervision was a focal point for learning to understand the work, and although both the learning and the work included so many factors that the task might seem too complex, there are two aspects worth noting. First, once workers began to understand ways of learning about their work and themselves in it, such learning was not limited to supervision but continued between sessions, and eventually without supervision. It was an approach to understanding and awareness which required help for some time, but which was not dependent on help indefinitely. Second, although concentration could be on one small aspect of the work (a small group, a relationship, the areas of authority or policy making), the insights and understanding resulting from the intensive study were frequently used and applied to other areas of work. Sometimes a worker related such insights of his own accord. Sometimes he needed help in doing so.

DIFFERENT APPROACHES TO LEARNING

It is obvious, however, that although this chapter has covered a wide range of learning, and this range was covered in supervision, the awareness of workers, the speed and directions in which they learned, and the areas which were understood, varied considerably. Workers were selective in what they learned, and in the ways in which they learned, depending on their previous knowledge, perception and experience. A worker (like everyone else) learned what he wanted to learn, but because of the nature of supervision, in doing so he found he wanted to learn more.

Because of the different approaches to learning, and the different ways in which workers learned in supervision, a summarised description follows of each worker learning in supervision. This points up the differences and some similarities. When workers read this description, they recognised themselves, but pointed out that they had also seen themselves in parts of descriptions of other workers. The description does not therefore provide a whole picture, but merely gives emphasis to certain factors.

An approach from personal difficulties

B, C and F began their learning by describing difficulties which they had in their work. There were two reasons – first, they were in difficulties; and second, they understood learning in supervision to be from problems. In supervision, the factors around the difficulties were examined and partially clarified. Aspects relating to adults, officials, volunteers, members, functions, etc., were explored in detail, together with some aspects of the worker's behaviour. In each case one part of the problem emerged as the worker's lack of understanding of her own role, and of the expectations and attitudes of other people. At different stages, each of the three workers became interested in the new range of information from which they could observe this, and found it a new incentive for learning. Each of the three started from an emotional state (of varying degree), moved on to a partial clarification of the situation and herself in it, and then began to think about her situation in a different way, and learn from it. None of these applied their understanding to theories for a long time, and then it was because the supervisor related these.

But with this common element, the workers proceeded to learn in different ways. F found it difficult to think when she was in trouble, though it was the development of situations which she did not understand which confused her and caused the trouble. Her learning, therefore, was first in clarifying a situation, and the supervisor was needed to recognise and accept the confusion,, and stimulate thought. This gave F an incentive to learn. When the problem was clarified and understood, she could learn for periods of increasing length about dif-

different aspects of her work, with or without problems. These were fruitful periods, in which structure, behaviour, role and recording were explored with understanding. During these periods, F gained insights into her own confusions, but it needed many months, during which this process was repeated several times, before F was able to stimulate herself, without outside help, into thinking while in difficulties.

F's learning was also scattered with sudden insights, and the satisfaction of gaining these was frequently followed by a struggle to use them. The insights were sometimes into her own behaviour, her feelings and values and their effect, and sometimes into other aspects of her work. As the different strands of her learning developed and merged – her increased intellectual understanding, her insights, and her recognition of the points at which she became confused – F eventually understood both her own strength and potential and also the reasons why she did not always think for herself. When these two became related, F became in control of her situation through understanding it, and her actions changed. Emotions could be dealt with and F's mind, which was always lively, was free to think. She was then able to concentrate on other people, to analyse, draw conclusions, and use insights with increasing rapidity.

C, in contrast to F, found it difficult to learn when she had no problems. When these occurred she explored them, and studied the factors which created the difficulties, including her own behaviour. Problems were her incentive for learning, and when they did not exist she merely enjoyed her work for periods, bringing into it her new insights. At such times she had no incentive to learn, understood that this was so, and said she wished she had assignments. The supervisor acted as a stimulus in suggesting choices, and on each occasion C learned for a period about her situation by exploring her observations of groups and incidents, gaining new insights and a wider range of information. But unless there was a new problem she was quickly satisfied again.

C's imagination was caught, however, when she began to supervise. Supervision presented a problem, because C had no experience of training, particularly an individual. It was a situation on which she had to concentrate, and which could not be easily set aside. As C explored supervision, she began to realise that there was a much wider range of information from which to learn, and was then able to use her feeling and thinking at a deeper level of understanding. She no longer needed the same stimulation in order to learn, and began to relate her insights to other aspects of her work, comparing supervision to other settings. It seemed that in the new setting of supervising, which required ongoing learning in order to understand what was happening and how she could help, that C was able to bring together a variety of unrelated learning from other settings.

B, who also started learning from the difficulties she had, learned to understand them by applying her thinking to them, but while accepting that she had feelings which affected her behaviour, found it more difficult to examine them and their effect. She was quickly able to understand the meaning of situations, and her incentive for learning became a desire to understand more about her work, individual and group behaviour, structures, recording, roles, attitudes and expectations. B was also an intuitive leader who understood the needs of young people and could describe and act towards them with feeling. She was methodical, prepared a great deal of material for long periods, and learned to relate practice to theories rapidly. This aspect of B's learning was interspersed with emotional situations, from which her learning was limited, because the problems were resolved mainly in terms of understanding outside factors. When B began to supervise, the contained setting of two people made it more possible for her to reflect on her own behaviour and its results, as well as on that of the other person. It was at this stage that B began to learn about and understand the situation, her role, and her behaviour, in relation to each other.

An individual approach – steady progress

A was prepared to learn in any way he could. He very much wanted guidance as to what and how he should learn, and was sometimes at a loss when he didn't get it. He was an accepting worker and learner as opposed to an assertive worker and learner. This meant that at least two factors were evident in his learning. First, he was able to learn from any situation or incident – all learning was useful, about groups, individuals, structure, society, role, recording. He was prepared to work in order to learn, to prepare material, and to co-operate in examining it, and he thought about it. Although this meant discomfort at times, most of the time he gained satisfaction from acquiring new understanding and a wider range of information from which to consider his work. His learning was a slow, methodical progression of developing insights, without extremes and with little emotion.

Alongside this was the second factor – A's learning how and when to assert himself. In order to do this he had to understand his own behaviour. In the early days awareness of this aspect could have led to less confidence and less ability to learn. The supervisor's attempts to leave the initiative to A resulted in silence, embarrassment, or a searching for something to say. A's learning about his own behaviour was possible only as his confidence in himself as worker and learner grew. When he saw that he had strengths in both settings and understood them, he was able to examine his own role in his work, in detail and from every aspect. Then he was able to see the points at which more initiative and assertion were required and the reasons for it. Learning about a difficulty in his own behaviour became possible at a stage in which he was confident in his ability both to learn and work, and it was absorbed into the steady progress of his other learning. The practice of supervising provided a valuable setting for this aspect of learning. A was already well able to accept and listen, and in a contained setting was quickly able to recognise the initiative he needed to take, and reasons why he was not taking it. Thinking about and understanding both these aspects resulted in his being able to take initiative not only in supervising, but in determining what he needed and wanted to learn about.

An individual approach – from a social problem

H almost always started his learning from a social problem – violence, drug-taking, immigration, housing, different approaches to youth work. These community situations were his starting points. To have pressed H to look at himself in relation to these problems might well have prevented him from learning. He moved slowly from a consideration of the implication of these problems for all concerned, to a point where he could look at his own responsibility in relation to them. This meant that his learning appeared to move in waves, starting at a wide problem and moving to himself. At this point he would look at himself until the next wave came along. The length of time in which he looked at himself and his responsibilities slowly increased.

Closely related to this approach to learning was the fact that H was intuitive. His intuition, his understanding of behaviour, feelings, and problems, through his own feelings, was developed to a high degree. He could describe situations with feeling and understanding. But this also meant that he tended to take his own action for granted – if something went wrong he would blame himself or some authority for not understanding. If something went right, he could take no credit – it was natural. An example of this was in racial integration. H objected to an attitude of benevolence towards immigrants, pointing out that given the right environment, young people integrated as a natural process. He gave as illustrations his own and other clubs and schools. It was only as he was asked to look at what he had done in his club that he was able

72

to see how many factors he had considered, how much understanding he had needed, and how many difficulties had to be overcome, and actions taken, to develop a multi-racial club.

H's learning began with attempts to examine complex situations, and find out where the problems lay; so he worked on documents about the needs of members and young people, and the problems and effects of drugs. Inevitably such study, which was of people, affected his own attitudes, understanding and actions, and in understanding more factors, H began to see how much he had to accept, and the points at which he could take action. But it was when H began to supervise that he found he had to concentrate indefinitely on his own actions – the situation was reduced to a confrontation with one person. At times he preferred to discuss supervision in general, and tried various ways of resisting analysing his supervision. But by this time he was aware of what he was doing, and he very much wanted to learn to analyse. Eventually he was able to do so.

The learning of the intuitive person can, therefore, be seen to vary. Whereas it might be expected that H's learning would be an effort to bring reasoning to bear on his intuitive actions, particularly within the club setting, in this instance it might well have been a limiting factor as it would have excluded a wide area of knowledge. The incentive to learn came partly from a desire for his contribution to be recognised, but mainly from a concern about many things which affected people. The satisfaction in learning came from building on or deepening the knowledge about this variety. The ability to look at and learn about his own behaviour came with the confidence of understanding the meaning of, and being able to deal with, many situations.

An individual approach – a limited use of supervision

K was a competent worker who had carried a complex job for some time. He learned much more away from supervision than he did within the sessions. This worked in two ways. First, as he was experienced, and used to observing and learning a great deal from his observations, he worked out as much as possible for himself before coming to a session. Second, when he reached a point in supervision when he became aware of a new idea or factor, he left it for further consideration when he was alone. He was therefore using supervision as a sounding board for his learning from his situation, and also as a source from which he could widen his range of information.

While this appeared helpful and was satisfactory to K during periods of stability in his work, when his complex situation erupted supervision was completely inadequate. K felt that he must work out his problems for himself. But this took so much time and effort that he missed several sessions at a time. During this period many actions were taken by K and his colleagues, and supervision, which was spasmodic, could be used only for superficial examination. Gradually the complications in his work increased, and except for two consultations, K did not come to sessions for eight months.

In another period of stability it was possible for K, in supervision, to examine what had happened. He understood how supervision had helped him (described above) and was able to work out areas in which he then realised he wanted to learn. He also recognised some of the implications for himself if he committed himself to this learning, which was mainly in training adults, and understanding himself in relation to them. Finally, K decided that he did not want to continue, although he continued to meet the supervisor for discussions from time to time, and participated in the group evaluation of the project.

An approach from intellectual learning

D, E, G and J wanted to learn through an intellectual discussion about their work. They wanted to 'know', to master their knowledge of their work without going through the process of learning. At the time the workers were unaware of this, and the supervisor saw it as a desire to learn, but to remain untouched in the process. Each one indicated that he wanted to know more about groups or recording. Otherwise they described their situations judgementally (though not necessarily critically), implied that they were in control of the situation and had no sense of inadequacy. Their learning started with an examination of their statements – opinions – on an incident, a group or the total setting, in order to find evidence from their observations. Each worker then searched for information, and realised the points at which he could substantiate statements, the points at which he needed more information, or the points at which he needed to understand other factors which had to be considered before making a statement. But each worker learned differently.

E, who was skilled in administration, organisation, and producing ideas, became interested in the possibilities of understanding more of what was happening in his work. Although this also showed him what he did not already know, the satisfaction of gaining knowledge overcame the annoyance that it was not already there. Much of his early learning was simply an increased awareness of what was happening. The complete destruction of E's premises affected his learning. From being learning. From being in a central position for youth work in the area, E found himself (having chosen to stay) in dilapidated premises where a large proportion of the members were anti-social. Involvement through close contact with members was the area of work which E had found difficult and evaded. But he spent months in this close contact, learning to understand the members, and himself and his helpers in relation to them. In doing so, E laid hiniself wide open to this new experience, and to examining it. His attitudes and understanding changed considerably. This experience was a mixture of satisfaction and strain, but E was able to accept it and use it in the same way as his earlier, more incidental learning. Eventually he applied it to the knowledge and ability which he already had, and integrated the two. E's learning therefore appeared to relate to his need to be intellectually in control of his knowledge, but he was prepared to go out on expeditions of learning, allowing things to happen to him, and bring back his insights.

When E began to supervise, he was able to explore the supervision with little difficulty, and he learned to understand the points at which he limited his expeditions, and the reasons for it. Another facet of E's learning was his use of analogies. He described the behaviour of some young people in primitive terms, supervision and his own behaviour in medical terms. As he was able to learn about his work through these analogies, so he learned to help other leaders, by relating their present experience to other experiences in their own background. While E used analogies more frequently than other workers, several workers found it a useful way of learning at different stages.

G's learning was of a 'staccato' nature. He wanted to master situations by understanding them in theory, to know how to supervise, how to record, preferably from books or an instructor. He tended to make snap judgements without his own evidence to substantiate theory. His interest in people and learning about them was aroused in his first supervisory session, when through questioning he realised that his own feelings, of which lie had been unaware, had affected an incident. From this point, G was in conflict between wanting to 'know' and wanting to 'understand'.

G's learning, therefore, could begin with his theories on an incident he had recorded, followed by an examination of the incident. He became frustrated by the examination, partly because it was so slow and partly because it frequently produced information which he felt he should already have known. When G gained new insight into some aspect of the incident he could concentrate only on that, until he understood what it meant for his work. This was followed by a period of depression because there was so much to learn. The whole process could take place in one session, but could also stretch over several weeks.

G also worked towards understanding theories in terms of reality – how did one recognise a self-programming group, how could he participate in a group and yet be objective about it, how could group achievement be recognised except in terms of an activity? Suddenly after a struggle, when observing a group, or in supervision, G found he could answer one of these questions in terms of people, and again he had a new insight. G learned, therefore, from two approaches: from examining his snap judgements in situations, and from trying to understand theories through his observations. It was difficult for G, with his quick mind, but it became easier when he understood what was happening in his learning, and when it became punctuated more frequently with insights from experience. He knew that he did not need to learn in this way, that he had other abilities which could be used in youth work, but he chose to continue, as he believed that in order to teach he needed to be able to learn from people as well as about them. With his growing awareness of himself his learning and his situation, G was able to extend his short, sharp bursts of learning so that he learned more deeply over longer periods.

J also wanted to know how to act, to supervise or to record, and at first it seemed that his learning was moving on lines similar to those of G. But he wanted theories from which to judge his work, from which to assess the rights and wrongs. In the early days he learned from the examination of incidents or situations, gaining increased awareness into what was happening. But as his idea of learning was to get answers as to what should be done, for a period he resisted learning from his experience, and spent time trying indirectly to persuade the supervisor to provide advice, information and theories. Two factors helped J to continue at this stage. First, he felt the supervisor must 'know' so it would be useful to find out what this knowledge was. Second, J's growing awareness about situations, and about himself in relation to learning, was proving useful and intrigued him. He therefore continued to present situations and learn from them, recognising eventually alongside other factors the impact upon them of his own values and feelings. This new recognition, though difficult to accept at first, started a new phase in J's learning. He became more relaxed, and in the examination of any incident was able to look at himself as one of the factors.

After a period, J's anxiety to be able to supervise came into conflict with his growing ability to learn from and analyse his work. He could not see how learning about his situation would help him to supervise, and he believed he should be able to supervise. He therefore started to supervise members of his own staff, for whose training he was already responsible. After a short period, during which J learned about his abilities and difficulties in supervising, he returned in his own supervision to learning more about himself in his work, and his own supervising became spasmodic. Eventually J became much more in control of his situation through his understanding of it. He then did not attend sessions for three months, after which he became aware that, whereas he was relaxed and in control of his work, he could not supervise. He realised how his urge to supervise had affected his learning and became clear as to what was happening. He then decided that he wanted to learn to supervise and that this would take time.

J's learning, therefore, was a slow process of learning from his situation, through examination and analysis, and included a growing awareness of himself as a factor in it. This reached a stage where he understood more clearly what was happening and what he was doing, thinking and feeling. But this process was hampered by J's desire at the same time to be in the position of 'knowing how'. He limited his understanding of learning to his own ability, and this prevented him from learning to relate one area of knowledge to another. It was only after he had practised supervising, which was what he felt he should be able to do, that he recognised how much more he wanted to learn about himself in his work – that he could not concentrate on another person's needs in learning while his own needs were so pressing.

D was similar to G in his approach, in that he wanted to learn theoretically, and to J in that he was prepared to learn from situations. He also found it difficult to accept that he had problems or weaknesses. He therefore used the supervisor as a sounding board, presenting material and discussing any aspect which she seemed prepared to explore without committing himself in any way. His first learning was in recognising that he had to make decisions as to what he wanted to learn, which meant accepting that he needed to learn about some aspect. During the first months, D picked up new ideas and became aware of new factors which could be considered in examining his work – he was widening the range of information with which to examine his work.

This method of learning, which D appreciated, might have continued indefinitely, but at the same time D constantly defended himself or described situations or ideas differently when he felt his original descriptions might be unacceptable, or when examination had shown him to have been unhelpful. At first D was unaware of this, and when he recognised that it was happening, did not know the reason, or how it could be changed. In an attempt to understand, he began to record – to commit himself in writing – and to learn from the records. For several months D continued to learn from records, understanding more about groups and individuals, particularly adults. But alongside this, D began to learn more about himself in relation to other people, and he realised his difficulty in listening to, and learning from, other people.

Then D, like J, decided he ought to supervise – that he was in a rut, and wanted to make progress. He decided to supervise members of his staff, but he did not do so. Instead he recorded staff meetings, and gained insight into different methods which could be used in such meetings. Then he stopped recording and began to study structure, policy, objectives, attitudes, areas of responsibility and decision making. As he did this, he studied himself in terms of his actions, behaviour and beliefs, instead of in terms of an image of himself. When he became able to accept this behaviour, he began to recognise, understand and accept feelings in himself and in other people. It was at this stage that he was able to start supervising, and to relate different areas of his knowledge.

Whereas earlier, D had seen behaviour in terms of either/or, being directive or permissive, good or bad, general or specific, and had found himself trying to go from one extreme to another, he began to understand what it meant to learn from a situation and act according to his learning from it. Although D's learning throughout had been from situations, it was only from an acceptance of, and an examination of, his own behaviour, values and feelings, that he was able to perceive new meaning in the situations. D's learning, therefore, started from an intellectual approach (with hidden feelings) and moved to learning about situations involving himself, to learning to recognise feelings and relate them to situations.

FINAL COMMENTS

There are perhaps several aspects of learning that could be noted here. First, that without dividing themselves into categories, some workers are more 'accepting' and some are more 'assertive'. The more accepting person finds it easier to learn from the situation than the more assertive person. The former wants to understand, and is prepared to listen, observe and think in order to do so. But frequently he needs more stimulation to think, analyse, act for himself, and take the consequence of his own actions. The latter wants to 'know', to be in control, to make his mark, and finds listening, observing and examination a frustration which prevents him from being quickly in the position of knowing. It is only when his imagination is caught by 'understanding' as opposed to 'knowing' that he is prepared to learn more slowly and from his situation. Even then it can be a long struggle to sort out the conflict in himself about learning. But the more accepting worker and the more assertive worker have each a great deal to offer, particularly when he understands his own ability, potential and behaviour. Experience in the project has shown that while basically the person might remain the same, he can learn to change his behaviour and participate differently. The more accepting worker can learn to assert himself when he sees the need, and can enjoy doing so. The more assertive person learns to listen, observe and understand, and finds new satisfaction in it.

While learning from and about the situation, the worker is looking outside himself, but is also becoming increasingly aware of his own behaviour feelings and values. Perhaps an important aspect of supervision is that it should help such learning to be an interesting process, rather than a deflating, unhappy one. Inevitably, increased awareness brings discomfort or depression at times, and workers would confirm this. But if learning from the situation is geared to building on to what a worker knows and is aware of, then the awareness of new factors to be recognised and understood can be gradual and acceptable; recognition of a weakness can be balanced with recognition of strength, understanding lack of a skill can be seen in terms of acquiring that skill.

The situation about which a worker is learning is complex, ranging round his community, and there is a great deal for him to learn about. His own behaviour is only one aspect of a situation, from which the opportunities for learning and increased effectiveness are unending. This means that from the point of view of supervision, a particular approach to learning can be used and developed, and any aspects can be chosen and explored. A function of supervision is to help any worker to learn from his situation in his own way and at his own pace, and to help him to relate at his own pace the three areas – the situation in which he is working, his role in that situation, and his behaviour as it affects it. The worker who explored one incident or group, and understood the behaviour within it, could in time use this understanding in terms of widening circles of relationships. The worker who studied and understood a small problem in his club could in time use this understanding in terms of community problems. The worker who studied a social problem could eventually understand the part he played within it in terms of his own relationships. No two workers learned in the same way, or covered the same ground, but there was the common element of situations, relationships, and relating these.

By the time workers learned to supervise through practice, they had increased their understanding of themselves and their work. For some, supervising was a continuation of learning, but in a different situation. For some, supervising provided a new incentive for learning. For some, the contained setting of two people increased the pace of this learning or made it possible to relate different aspects. For others, the responsibility of supervising came too soon, and they found their own ways of learning according to their needs, even though they supervised. Some workers found that they began to understand their own work more clearly through helping supervisees to learn about theirs.

This was a period in which workers were learning a new skill, and the ways in which they did so will be described in Chapter 10. But just as they had earlier applied insights to different situations, so eventually workers found themselves applying their skill, which they had acquired in supervising, to their work with their own staff and volunteers, and to group training which they undertook in other settings.

CHAPTER SEVEN

Skills and Techniques – Definition and Setting

DEFINITION

SKILLS are understood as knowing how to do something, or the practised ability to do something, and techniques as the manner of execution – the methods used to achieve a purpose. Thus, in specific terms, if the purpose were to help a worker examine his own statement, the skill is the ability to help him do so, and the techniques used are sometimes questions in different forms. It might be useful to consider, first, essential factors in acquiring skill, and later, how skills and techniques could be used.

FACTORS TO BE CONSIDERED

It is impossible to consider skill in isolation – to be learned from books or lectures. It can be acquired only in relation to other factors, some of which are described here. Skill requires concentration on someone or something outside oneself, and a willingness to learn from that someone or something. It also requires contact, and the practice of techniques which need to be tried and examined in terms of their usefulness. Finally, it requires a knowledge and acceptance of a purpose and basic principles, the context in which the skill is bring practised.

A batsman acquires skill mainly through concentration on the bowler and the ball. It is important that he should learn what the bowler is trying to do, how he performs, and the ways in which the ball is likely to come through the air. Different bowlers mean new learning for the batsman. While concentrating and learning, the batsman has to practise numerous techniques in holding his bat and hitting the ball. One technique used for a particular ball from a particular bowler could mean a boundary; the same technique applied to a different ball from the bowler could mean an end to his innings. But cricket is not merely a game between batsman and bowler. The batsman is playing within a particular setting: he understands the purpose and rules of the game, and not only understands but accepts them. He has a conviction as to their value within the sphere of sport and entertainment.

The skill of a craftsman or mountaineer can be considered in the same way. The craftsman concentrates on his material and learns about its texture and possibilities. He practises on it through manipulation or the use of tools. He wants to produce a useful or beautiful article, and understands the function of tools and the properties of material and can relate this knowledge to finished articles. The mountaineer concentrates on a particular mountain, learning about its structure and peculiarities. He believes in the value of climbing. He practises footholds and handholds, but he also understands and accepts the effects of weather, the equipment needed, and the opportunities and limitations of mountaineering. All these skills therefore relate to a purpose, to concentration outside oneself, a willingness to learn from something outside oneself, practice of techniques through constant contact, and an understanding and acceptance of the context in which they are being practised.

Skill in supervision requires acknowledgement of the same factors. First, the supervisor needs to understand the setting in which his skill is used. Second, he recognises that his skill is dependent on his ability to concentrate on the supervisee, and his willingness to learn from the supervisee about the supervisee and his work. Third, the supervisors contact with the supervisee is through verbal communication, and he needs to practise different techniques in communication, to examine these, and learn which are helpful and appropriate at which times. Fourth, he needs a conviction about, and an acceptance of, supervision as one form of training.

Understanding the setting

The previous chapters have described the setting in which the supervisor uses skill. The order of presentation was not by chance, but was decided upon because skill can be developed and used only in relation to, and with an understanding of, all the factors. These include: first, the basic assumptions as to the needs, the approach, the methods and the purpose; second, the context in which supervision takes place – the youth service; third, the setting of supervision – the relationship – with feelings, attitudes, expectations, the functions of the supervisor and the contributions of the supervisee, which determine the potential of the relationship; fourth, the content of supervision, the material to be discussed, brought by the supervisee; fifth, the supervisee as a learner – the ways in which he could learn, and the means which he is able to use in order to learn. Skill in supervising requires an acknowledgement and understanding of this setting.

Concentrating on the supervisee

The supervisor's skill is dependent on his ability to concentrate on, and learn from, the supervisee. It is the supervisee who will express his needs or indicate what they are; who will bring material or not know what to bring; who will indicate what he feels, what he expects, and what he can contribute to or take from the relationship; who will indicate his ability to learn, and the areas in which he is prepared and able to learn. It is in concentrating on the supervisee that the supervisor learns what to expect from him, and the techniques which will be most helpful to him.

Practising techniques

Although supervision requires the constant use of techniques, they can be used effectively only in relation to all the factors previously described. Their value can be ascertained not in isolation, but from examination of the supervisee's need at any particular moment, the purpose of the discussion, the helpfulness of the technique to the supervisee, and all of these in relation to previous knowledge.

For example, two supervisees might come in at different times, saying, 'Everything is in a mess'. The first has a very demanding job with which he is coping, and finds it very difficult to express his feelings about it – he might be unable to do so easily, or believe it is disloyal to do so. The response, 'Are you feeling worried about it?', or 'What is worrying you about it?' might provide the outlet needed by the supervisee at that moment. The second supervisee also has a demanding job, but constantly deplores his situation, finding this easier than thinking about it. The same questions would encourage this inclination, but alternatives, depending on the stage of the relationship, could be, 'So what are you going to do about it?', 'Let's look at it', or 'You often think of things as being in a mess, don't you?' Such an example merely illustrates the futility of trying to acquire or use techniques without a good deal of information.

Conviction about the purpose, approach and methods

It might seem obvious that a supervisor needs to be convinced about the purpose he is trying to achieve, and the approach and methods he uses. But as this calls for a particular attitude of mind, it is not necessarily easy. For example, in a youth work setting, it is perhaps more widespread to believe that one's authority (be it in knowledge or in imposing discipline) comes by reason of one's official appointment (training and/or experience being implicit in this). In supervising (training and/or experience accepted) it could be said that one's authority comes from an ability to learn from the situation, and to accept another person, and then to develop skills to help him. Without being exclusive, in the first, the emphasis is on the past and oneself, and in the second, it is on the present and another person. (The same as the worker learning from the situation in the previous chapter.)

Another example is that one either does or does not accept the principle that a supervisor helps the supervisee to think or learn to think for himself. If one does, one is prepared to move along at a pace determined by the supervisee's ability to think, sometimes a slow one. If one does not, one hands out advice as to how he should cope with his work. Accepting different principles usually calls for changes in attitude − relatively easy for some, more painful for others. Experience in the project showed that some workers had to change attitudes in order to supervise, and for two or three it required a long period of learning, practice, and reappraisal.

AN OUTLINE OF SKILLS AND TECHNIQUES

In the project, skill was seen as a practised ability to supervise, taking into consideration all the factors described, and techniques were seen as the different means used by the supervisor to achieve its purpose. It could also be said that skill in supervising was an ability to select and use appropriate methods for achieving a purpose, and the techniques were the methods. But the overall skill in supervising also required a particular combination of simple skills. There were several skills, which together formed skill in supervision. These, as understood in the project, are now presented in an outline.

1. Skill − the ability to learn from the worker about himself and his work.
   Techniques − observing, listening, questioning.
2. Skill − the ability to assess needs (to use the knowledge acquired from learning and to know when and how to use it).
   Techniques − observing, listening, questioning, relating knowledge to previous knowledge, analysing and drawing conclusions.
   − recording sessions, analysing records, drawing conclusions, and relating these to other records.
3. Skill − the ability to convey acceptance and support of the worker.
   Techniques − listening, paying attention, using words which recognise the feelings and problems expressed, or which help a worker think about himself and his situation at the point from which he wants to go.
4. Skill − the ability to help a worker to learn.
   Techniques − questioning, exploring statements, reflecting, exploring a situation,

suggesting choices, drawing out more information, more factors, crystallising, summarising, relating, conceptualising, using records.
– questioning in order to help the worker use all these techniques for himself.

There are two points to be noted here. First, the skill is that which cannot be seen or heard, but the technique is that which can be seen or heard. Second, although skill is separated from skill, and technique from technique in this outline, when used by people and in terms of people, they cannot be isolated in the same way. 'Recognising feelings' could convey acceptance, but could also be a means of helping a worker to learn. 'Exploring a statement' could be used to help a worker to learn, and also as a means of learning for the supervisor. Isolating the concepts is therefore an artificial process, and seems valid only if the purpose is to understand each one, and see how they relate to each other. This is a process similar to that described in Chapter 5, when a subject was isolated, examined and related again.

CHAPTER EIGHT

Skills and Techniques – How they were applied

THE ABILITY TO LEARN FROM THE WORKER

THE supervisor's learning from the specific contributions of a worker in the early stages of supervision was described fully in Chapter 4. But there are other aspects of learning worth noting.

From his point of view

In the first place, the supervisor was dependent on the worker for her learning about his situation – she heard about it from his point of view. If a worker indicated that all was well with his adult relationships and that he wanted to explore particular groups of members, this was the limit of the supervisor's learning unless, or until, some other factors emerged. It was inevitable that some situations were already known to the supervisor from other sources, but she was not there to help the other sources, and she wanted to understand how the worker felt about it, and what he saw in it. A conflict of opinion between the worker and an official of his organisation or the youth officer was bound to emerge in time if the worker wanted help with it, and if the supervisory relationship were sound. That would be, and was, the time when conflicting opinions were explored. To help the worker then, the supervisor wanted to learn about the situation as he described it.

Through concentration

The supervisor needed to concentrate on the worker, to have her mind open to what he was saying, and doing, so that she could understand what he needed at any given time. Perhaps the most apt illustration of this is one in which the supervisor was not concentrating.

EXAMPLE

F and E were both practising supervision. F came for her session with S in the morning. E followed her in the afternoon. In the morning session, F examined how she had worked with her own supervisee, and became interested in the resources which she had to use in order to be helpful. S questioned her so that F slowly described the different areas of knowledge she was using – several from her basic training, from her understanding of basic principles in supervision, and from the worker she was supervising. This was the first time F had been concerned about these factors, and she commented that relating them helped her to see the sense in supervising. She went on to relate other factors in her own work and found it an interesting exercise.

In E's session, he said he was not sure what he had done in his supervisee's session. He thought he had been helping with the wrong problem. The record was explored, the problems clarified, and S asked which problem the supervisee had presented.

E The group.

S What did you find out about the group?

E Very little. I should have got much more information.

S For what purpose?

E So that I could help him to see that it was there, and use it. There should have been a searchlight on the group.

S What do you think blocked the light?

E (a) I was concerned about this other problem (professionalism). (b) I didn't try to learn about the group. (c) We hadn't much time. The trouble is that I don't know what questions to ask about groups.

S Sometimes the questions are very simple, and might seem too elementary.

E Sometimes X uses words without looking at the meaning. I could have explored these.

S Where do you get your knowledge from which to ask questions?

E Training and experience.

At this point S tried to help E explore this statement, to consider areas of knowledge used. When he was unable to do so, she made suggestions about it. She suddenly realised that E was looking very tired and weary, so she said:

S This is irrelevant. I am on the wrong line. X has a problem about his groups, and you want to know what questions you can ask X in order to get information about the groups. Let me give you a simple example of this. I read recently of a worker who told her supervisor that she was worried because she couldn't make herself like a particular girl, Mary. The supervisor simply said to her, 'Tell me about Mary'.

E Of course, I could simply say, 'Tell me about the groups'. If you had used that example at the beginning I should have understood immediately.

S I was attempting too much.

E But that's what I did. I've been shooting off to him at eighty miles an hour and hoping I would solve it. If I'd kept to the simple stuff I might have helped him do the same.

E's weariness had disappeared.

Comments

S used a technique, drawing out factors to help F relate knowledge. She knew that F was ready for this – the technique and subject related to her need at that moment. But later when E was trying to understand his situation, instead of concentrating on him, S remembered the morning's success, and decided to use the same technique, directing the subject. She was thinking about her own ideas. Not only did she try the same technique, but when E could not co-operate, she answered herself. E's expression pulled her up sharply, and she realised what she was doing, and said so, and used a simple technique of offering an example which related to his need at that moment. An interesting factor which emerged was that E had made the same mistake. He had been concerned with his ideas Instead of concentrating on X. He saw this more speedily than S and found his own solution.

Hearing what was not said

The supervisor learned about the worker, and his situation, not only from what he said and did and from his expression, but also from factors underlying what he said. 'I believe in self-determination' could be said in different ways, and the supervisor could wonder if a worker were talking about members, or his own difficulties with his management committee. The supervisor learned therefore from what was not said, in terms of expression and attitudes. But this was a slower process. Snap judgements would rarely have been usefully used.

EXAMPLE

F, who described in a confused way the differing expectations of adults and young people in her situation, was, to the supervisor, obviously confused by them – but the supervisor did not know why. The techniques at that point were questions which helped F to clarify the expectations, the attitudes and the parts played by individuals and groups, one by one. The problem had to be sorted out as presented. The supervisor was thus learning more about the situation and the people involved in it, and helping F at the same time.

But the supervisor was also asking herself the questions – Why is F confused? Is it because the situation is impossible to work in? Is it because she has not known how to clarify it? Is it because she prefers to opt out – to apportion blame and not think about herself? Assumptions could be made, but the answers could not be known at once. To have asked the question, 'Why are you confused?' of someone presenting a confused situation would in the first place have added to the confusion, and in the second it could have implied that F was to blame. The supervisor could only continue with the material presented, helping F to see what was causing the confusion, and keeping her questions in mind.

After three sessions it became clear that the situation was indeed complex, in which adults related in a variety of ways inside and outside the club setting, unable to clarify what should happen in the club. F said, having been able to take limited action to help the adults, that she knew she tended to opt out and stop thinking if things seemed too difficult. It was at this point that F's opting out was discussed, and it was then possible to recognise it openly as a factor to be considered in future discussions.

In this instance, and constantly, the supervisor was learning from what the worker said and did, and also from inward questioning of what was not necessarily said and done. The importance of this way of learning was not that it happened – it would seem inevitable – but what was done with such knowledge. It could be a temptation to state the knowledge immediately or to gear all discussion so that it had to be said. But the supervisor's assumption could be wrong, and, if right, would not necessarily be helpful to new learning about the worker. If the material presented were explored each time, and if the supervisor were open to new learning and questions, eventually she would be able to recognise the moment when she could help a worker to understand a behaviour difficulty for himself, without it being a shattering experience.

Questioning statements

A third way of learning was from questioning statements. Frequently this was related to judgements and opinions. If the worker said his club was successful, or the management committee was hopeless, or that he believed you should trust people, the supervisor sometimes accepted that at its face value, particularly if the worker wanted to explore something else. But the supervisor could not be helpful if she merely listened to such opinions without understanding what they meant to the worker, and so she asked what he meant by successful, hopeless or trusting. Obviously this was also a technique for helping workers to explore their own values and judgements, or to provide factual evidence, but it also helped the supervisor to learn more about the workers. One worker might believe that a 'good' youth officer remained in his office and was available for advice or information when necessary. Another might believe a 'good' youth officer should visit regularly and get involved with the membership. Such subjective statements taught the supervisor something about the worker's attitudes to his own status or to professional relationships, or his feelings about a particular personality, and these could become a point for further discussion.

Such questioning was sometimes irritating to a worker – it seen-led like a return to the alphabet. Occasionally a worker who wanted supervision to be an exchange of opinions, resisted exploration, and the subject was changed, or the supervisor had to point out the reality of her own situation, that it would be difficult for her to help him look at his work if he had already judged it, and was not prepared to put his judgement into words she could understand.

Motives for learning

There were numerous ways of learning, and others are indicated in illustrations, but one more point could be mentioned here. It was important that the supervisor understood her motives for her learning. Sometimes, in this setting where a second person was accepting and obviously willing to listen, a worker wanted to talk about various aspects of his life, past and present, which were not related to his work. Sometimes the supervisor felt curious about an irrelevant aspect. In either case the supervisor had to recognise what was happening, and remind herself, and sometimes the worker too, that the purpose of the worker's contribution and her own learning was to help the worker in the work he was doing.

THE ABILITY TO ASSESS NEEDS

Basically, the supervisor had to develop her skill in assessing the worker's needs and his ability to learn, in the same way as the worker was developing his skill with members, although her purpose was more narrowly defined as training. She too needed to be listening more than talking, observing more than demonstrating, participating more than organising, drawing out more than imposing. She too had to withdraw, examine the factors in a supervisory session, relate them to her knowledge, think about them, analyse them, draw conclusions, assess needs and take action. It was only as a result of acting in these two areas, with the worker and away from him, that she was able to understand how and when a worker could be helped, and the ways in which he was prepared and able to accept help.

Although in generalised form the assessment of needs and ability sounds a complicated procedure, in practical terms it was based oil an accumulation of simple observations and communications. When H presented information about his club setting in the form of a social problem, the supervisor could recognise his intuitive ability and also his skill in describing pictorially. A few tentative questions as to how he understood his role in this setting brought out his feelings about it. His need to learn to be analytical and concise became clear immediately. But alongside this was needed an understanding of how H could and would learn. The way in which H described his work – with bravado, with humour, and sometimes in simple terms – indicated both his understanding and his need for confidence in himself. A question to be asked was, 'Would H learn to be analytical when he had more confidence, or would learning to be analytical give him more confidence?' The answer to both appeared to be 'Yes' and, as was usual, H worked his own way through, as long as the supervisor looked out for moments at which she could help him to develop his confidence, and points at which she could help him to analyse. The seminar training, which was mainly about group behaviour, was quickly absorbed by H and used to provide another way of describing his work. In recognising this ability to relate theory and practice the supervisor was then able to help H to use it, and thus to develop his confidence and analytical approach.

Frequently, in choosing to help a worker according to one need, another had to be excluded temporarily. A, who needed to develop his ability to take initiative, also needed confidence. In the earlier sessions, the supervisor made several suggestions as to material he might present or aspects he could observe. At this point she was working towards the development of confidence in himself, but in making the suggestions was not helping him to develop his initiative. B could record groups with skill, and spent a number of sessions exploring them mainly intellectually. Although the supervisor believed that B needed to understand more about her own involvement and feelings, at that point she chose to go along with B's need to widen her range of information about groups.

Similarly, on occasions when workers arrived saying they weren't sure why they had come to a session, as they had no material to discuss, the supervisor had to try to distinguish between the worker who had some reason for coming of which he was not aware, and the worker who believed the supervisor would think of something. In both instances the supervisor's action – drawing out – might well have been the same, but in the second, the supervisor knew that in taking the initiative she was not at that moment helping the worker to think for himself.

These and other constantly recurring examples were of making choices. Sometimes mistakes were made. These were usually when the supervisor had misjudged the worker's need of the moment (when lie quickly could bring the discussion back to his need), or when she tried to stretch him too far (when he became depressed, confused or annoyed). But mistakes could be retrieved when they were understood. In making these choices, the supervisor frequently noted two things.

First, she remembered that her role was a limited one, compared with the total area of the worker's learning – he would learn many things without her. Second, she was aware that a slow development in one aspect of learning could, at a given moment, provide an insight which a worker would quickly relate to many other aspects of his learning – in other words, one need could be met while another was being dealt with.

In describing the supervisor's assessment of needs, it might be implied that a worker was not choosing what he wanted to learn. It is important therefore to recognise the difference between subject matter and other factors in learning. A worker could very quickly determine the subjects he wanted to learn about, but it was less likely that he was aware of his inability to use his feelings, of his difficulty in relating theory and practice. Most of the needs which have been described were those of which he was unaware, or which he was unable to describe, and the supervisor needed skill not only in assessing these needs and helping the worker to meet them, but in helping him at the most appropriate time to become aware of them. The techniques essential to assessing needs were therefore numerous. While with the worker, they were observing, listening, questioning and helping him express himself, relating what was heard to previous knowledge, and drawing conclusions. When away from the worker, they were recording sessions, analysing records, drawing conclusions and relating these to other sessions.

THE ABILITY TO CONVEY ACCEPTANCE AND SUPPORT

The supervisor's acceptance was based on the principle that the worker was a person with his own feelings, attitudes, expectations, strengths, weaknesses, ideas, skills and knowledge, and his own understanding and ability in his job – and that he had a right to these. Her acceptance was first, then, an attitude of mind.

Attention to what a worker was saying, in itself was a way of communicating this attitude. A worker soon knew if the supervisor was waiting to make a point, or was thinking about something else. When the supervisor was listening, interested and relaxed, the worker felt that he was important to the discussion, and that there was plenty of time to express himself as he wanted or was able to do. From the beginning, then, acceptance was active, not passive or neutral.

The supervisor's support was based on the knowledge that the worker did not want to remain static – or he would not have come to supervision. He wanted to understand some things more clearly. In some areas he wanted to change, in other areas he was in conflict, and wanted help in understanding what he wanted to change, and what he wanted to do. She accepted him, therefore, as the person he was, with the potential he had, and supported him, not only as that person doing what he was doing, but in changing at the points at which he wanted to change, or in helping him find out what he wanted to change.

Conveying acceptance and support to the worker meant first that the supervisor accepted statements, ideas and feelings, without emotional reaction, without argument, and without comments of approval or disapproval. But she also used comments which showed that she recognised how he was feeling, or which accepted that this was what he believed at the moment, and he wanted no further discussion. This was why, when a worker, after describing an incident, said, 'The chairman was wrong in what he did', the response was, 'Was he?' and/or, 'Where do you believe he went wrong?', or, 'You sound upset by his behaviour'. The responses varied according to the way in which the statement was made, and to any indication whether the worker would continue. When a worker said, 'The management committee is hopeless', the response could have been, 'is it?' or, 'What's wrong with it?' or, 'Is it that you are feeling hopeless about it?' In this instance it could well have been true that a part of the worker believed what he said, and that part of him was saying, 'Help me to understand and work with this committee' or, 'Help me to get out of this situation'. A response was needed which could open up a discussion in which the worker's requirements could come to light. If the worker did not want to talk about it, he could indicate this, and the subject would be closed, but he had some reason for making the statement.

When a worker could express how he felt, the problem that he had, or the subject he wanted to discuss, conveying acceptance and support was comparatively simple. The supervisor could help him to look at the area suggested. But it was when the worker did not know, or was not sure, that the supervisor had to take care not to direct him towards considering something which she thought he ought to understand, instead of helping him to see for himself where he wanted to go. Frequently, in the early days, this was what a worker preferred. He wanted the supervisor to tell him what he needed to learn, or to take the initiative in discussing something, so that afterwards he could decide whether or not it was useful. Sometimes he wanted the supervisor's judgement on himself and his work – was he right or wrong? was it good or bad? Then he would be able to try to fulfil the supervisor's expectations, or argue about them, or just think about them.

93

The supervisor accepted that this was what the worker wanted, and had to help him to understand it too. But she also had to convey, sometimes by not taking on the role he expected, or by taking up his questions and reflecting them back to him, and sometimes by explanation, that it was his opinion, his feeling and thinking which mattered, and that she did not want, nor was prepared to try, to mould him or to be another authority for him to accept or kick against. This was seen as a step towards the worker's acceptance of himself, his independence of outside opinions, and his ability to consider his own behaviour objectively. In itself, it might be seen as a directive in the worker's learning, but it related to principles in his basic training as a youth leader, and also in supervision, which part of him accepted. He already wanted these things, but sometimes objected to methods of achieving them, in which the acceptance and support (as described) of a supervisor was a part.

Conveying acceptance and support was active, therefore, not only in that it expressed an attitude of mind, and helped a worker to understand what he was and was doing, and where he wanted to change, to learn more, or act differently, but it was also a tool in helping a worker accept himself, become independent, and learn to be objective. In an atmosphere where he was not judged, nor told what he should be or do, a worker found it increasingly easy to talk about some aspects of his work with which he was not satisfied (or the opposite), and in relation to this, to describe some aspects of his own behaviour, or express some feelings which did not satisfy, and sometimes worried him. Some of these things he had been trying to deny, which resulted in tensions, in putting on a front, or in blaming himself for anything that happened.

Usually after testing out supervision, a worker tentatively brought in a situation, behaviour difficulty, or feelings, about which he was uncertain. One worker described staff meetings, which he knew were not effective, and explained the reasons in terms of staff expectations, lack of time, and staff relationships. Underneath he believed he was wrong somewhere, and indicated this only by the way he talked and comments such as, 'I don't know what to do about it'. Exploration of the situation brought out that he always had to explain what should or must be done, that he disliked discussing a subject when he did not feel knowledgeable about it, and that the staff had little opportunity to participate fully. The worker said he did not want this to happen but did not know how to change it.

When this, and similar situations, were explored in the same way as situations where the worker felt in control, first he was relieved that it was in the open, and second, he began to accept that weaknesses and strengths were a part of him. For some workers this was one of the hardest aspects of learning, but in time a worker realised that in differing ways they always would be a part of him and that he could learn about, change and use both. Obviously, this was also an ongoing process; total acceptance and total awareness would be hard to find. But even a little was a medium for relaxed learning, objectivity and independence. The supervisor's acceptance md her communication of it helped to make the supervisory situation a medium for learning of this kind.

EXAMPLE

J talked a great deal in his first session about his total situation and the difficulties it presented, but described it as if he were able to cope with it satisfactorily. From the way he talked, S decided that he wanted confirmation that lie was doing well. She did not give this, but through questioning helped J to develop some of the complexities. In the following sessions, J presented groups for discussion, and interaction between group members was considered. J realised at the end new possibilities in working with groups which did not have a set activity. He said, 'I have only seen groups as activity groups before'. He sounded pleased to have learned this, but he also shook his head sadly. S believed that J had mixed feelings about being able to learn, and realising he had more to learn, and she suggested this. In his next session J discussed some of his difficulties in learning. He said that previously he had learned from people by talking to them, hearing where he was right or wrong, and receiving advice and information. S agreed that it could be difficult for him to learn from looking for himself at his situation, and aspects of his difficulties were discussed. He described his football group, and how he helped it, saying he could do so because he was an expert and the group knew he was. He wondered how one could help a group otherwise. Possibilities were discussed, but J said he knew that his difficulty was that he had to 'know'. S helped him to look at what he had to know and why he had to know it. J then went on to discuss his worries about his work, seeing these as a result of other people making it difficult for him. In the next session he continued this, and S asked what he felt these people were doing to him. J said, 'Preventing me from doing my job effectively'. 'Which means?' 'I can't be the good leader I want to be.' 'Do you think that being a good leader means being a perfect leader?' 'I know it isn't, but I know that I want to be the perfect leader.' 'Perhaps recognising that you are struggling for the impossible is useful.' Over a long period in which he looked at aspects of his work with which he could cope, and those which he found difficult, and became more aware of some of the feelings he had about work and people and himself, J began to accept himself and his behaviour in a more realistic way, that is, with a greater awareness of both strengths and weaknesses. Instead of shaking his head, he smiled when on occasions he was unable to do anything with his awareness. At times he went from one extreme

95

to another. A polite person, after recognising and accepting that he had feelings of anger, he expressed it forcefully. Having exercised strict control, he allowed staff to determine for themselves work in their own area, and did not always see the help they needed. After accepting that he needed to look at his own situation in order to learn and becoming dependent on supervision for a period while learning this way, he exerted independence and didn't come to supervision for three months. But it was possible for J to understand what had happened and to use the experience to develop his learning. His demanding and complex job continued to exist, but he approached it differently and became in control of it through understanding it. In doing so, he began to accept colleagues and their behaviour with more understanding.

Comments

S believed that J needed to present to other people, and himself, the idea that he was a 'good' leader, in control of his work. He therefore had to struggle to live up to this image, which meant an attempt to deny weaknesses. If S had expressed approval of his 'good' work at the beginning she would merely have strengthened J's need to present this image. When she did not do so, he brought out some of his difficulties – S being one, as she was making it difficult for him to learn. S accepted this, and his difficulties in it. S supported J in discussing with him any aspect which he wanted to discuss, and leaving it at the point at which J wanted to leave it. She recognised feelings which he expressed, and sometimes helped him to express them. Apart from this, J did a lot of thinking between sessions, and worked out many things for himself. Gradually he became more able to accept his situation and himself, and became a more relaxed person, able to accept more from other people.

It was not a smooth passage, particularly as he obviously had to meet the ongoing demands of his work while looking at himself in it. Sometimes he felt he was being pressured or changed against his will – which was true in that he wanted lectures, opinions and advice, and also supervision. In order to use supervision, he had to accept a different way of learning, that the supervisor's offering was limited and that she could not meet all his demands.

THE ABILITY TO HELP A WORKER TO LEARN

Obviously, learning from the worker, assessing needs, and conveying acceptance and support, were all means of helping a worker to learn. But in addition, techniques were used to help a worker understand more clearly the material he presented. Only those used most frequently in the project have been mentioned - questioning, exploring statements and situations, reflecting, suggesting choices, drawing out more factors, relating, summarising, crystallising, conceptualising. All of these were geared to helping a worker think, feel, analyse, draw his conclusions and make his own decisions.

The helping techniques used are difficult to illustrate for two reasons. First they have little meaning out of the context of the worker's total learning, of his needs at the moment in relation to other needs, and of the stage of his relationship with the supervisor. Second, techniques were not 'set pieces'. Numerous techniques were used in rapid succession in order to help with one particular aspect of learning – the supervisor could question, reflect what a worker had said, relate, and suggest choices within a very short period. As the techniques were in the form of verbal communication, presumably anything that was said could be described as a technique. Therefore, illustrations of specific techniques have a limited value – namely as a means of explaining what as meant by the words used to describe them. For this reason, only five are presented here, but reference to techniques will be made in records following, and others are to be found in the next chapter.

EXAMPLE 1

EXPLORING A STATEMENT

K said that X, who had previously been a volunteer, had now been appointed as full-time worker. K said that of course they would now be equals. S asked K what he meant by 'equals', and K's first answer was 'He'll be responsible when I'm not there'. S asked how this was equality. K then gave several reasons why X should be seen to have responsibility. S said that she understood how X's change of status was a factor to be considered, but she still didn't understand 'equality'. For instance, was X's signature being added to K's on the circular letter that K was sending out? K said no – X hadn't got to that stage of being equal – it might not be a bad idea for X to sign, though. S said she had not meant to imply that X should sign it, but was trying to find out what K meant by equality. By this time K was showing that he thought S was making a fuss about nothing, but S asked if he had considered the implications of 'equality'. K thought it would sort itself out. S reminded him of a seminar discussion when one worker had wanted to finish a discussion on roles in supervision by saying supervision was between two equals. K said this was irrelevant as supervision was not between two equals. S pointed out that one worker had been adamant about it. K then began to ponder on what he meant and what would happen to X and himself, and finally said, 'It is a question of inter-changeability', and 'We both have different areas of ability, and these must be used'. S suggested that K was now describing 'equality' in particular terms. K said, 'I know. I probably have reasons I don't understand, for emphasising the word "equality". I must think about it – but I suppose the important thing is that we discuss our work regularly and consider each situation.' S said she was wondering if he and X had the same ideas about X's position. What would X expect from 'equality'? K said he realised this could be a difficulty – X had already started to tell a volunteer what to do. The volunteer had said, 'You are starting to criticise me', and X had said, 'I'm a professional worker now'. K then continued to develop the incident with the volunteer.

97

Comments

K preferred giving opinions to examining a situation. He frequently made statements which he had not thought through and became exasperated and found himself in difficulties when people did not understand him. S felt that K must have some reason for his forceful comment and tried various techniques to persuade K to think about what he was saying – a testing out of his meaning (letter), an illustration (seminar), the reality (it had implications). When K began to think about his meaning, he realised for himself that he must have some reason for clinging to the word. S knew that once K understood this he would go back and work on it himself. The incident confirmed her earlier assumptions that K had some difficulty about authority relating to adults and he probably needed to sort it out. But her understanding of this was still vague.

EXAMPLE 2

REFLECTING

K began by describing a group of boys, saying that his role had changed with th group during the last weeks. At first he had been an authority to the boys, ensuring that their behaviour was not destructive within the building. A volunteer had worked with the group inside and outside the building, and with K's agreement had quoted K to the boys as the authority, whenever he felt he needed support. K said he had been very surprised when the boys changed fairly suddenly and began to tell him in great detail about their illegal escapades. He said he had done very little about it as he knew they were well aware of the possible consequences of their behaviour, and condemning their behaviour would also not have helped. He hoped the warmer weather and the diversions he was arranging would stop the escapades, but he was worried.

S suggested that they should look at what had happened in his relationship with the boys. What had happened when he was the authority figure? K said that an authority had been needed, that he and the volunteer agreed that they should take these separate roles and see what happened. The boys had tested K to the limit. S asked what was different in this second phase. K said he was now involved with society as well as the boys, and he wasn't sure where his loyalties lay. S agreed that a -oral problem had now arisen, and asked if he had ideas as to what would happen if he continued to listen, without pointing out consequences and without condemning. K thought the boys might begin to ask his help. S said that presumably if this were to happen, he was not doing 'nothing' about it, but was maintaining a relationship until he could do 'something' practical. K then remembered, and produced, examples of boys who had already asked his help. These were discussed, and K said he thought he might wait to find out the results of his present behaviour with the boys. S agreed that he would then have evidence to help him if he were in the same situation again.

At the end of the session K said, 'I can understand what I am doing with that group now. If you had come down strongly on my being wrong, I would have accepted it because I was so worried.'

Comments

K had a problem. He was worried because he felt he was standing aside when he knew that the boys were removing property, etc. As a citizen he felt a responsibility about it. He did not state the problem, nor was S aware of it until the middle of the discussion. K merely described something he wanted to look at – his reason was obscure. S helped K to describe the situation again in terms of 'what was happening when'. In this description the problem emerged. S acknowledged the problem, but continued to help K in the description. When he understood what he was doing, and that his behaviour might well prove to be constructive, K's original problem (values), though not resolved, was seen in a different light.

'Reflecting' was used in this incident in two ways – first, through asking questions, which helped K to think again and describe the situation differently; second, through repeating his words, or that which his words implied, in a new form. This technique uncovered a problem which K had been unable to state earlier. It also provided a leisurely teaching process because, by reason of its repetition, K was able to do his own thinking at his own pace.

EXAMPLE 3
DRAWING OUT MORE INFORMATION

D described a group of boys in the club, which he said was interesting. Each individual in the group was discussed in terms of his relation to the others, and his role in the group. D then said one boy, Jim, was being led astray by the others, but he was helping him, as Jim came alone on Saturdays to do odd jobs for D. When he was with the others in the club, Jim was liable to get into mischief. D said lie thought Jim was beginning to see the futility of this because one Saturday he asked Jim to clear up some rubbish left by the group on the Friday evening. D said 'I pressed it home at the time'. S asked about the boy's age, interests and background, and it emerged that he was an only child of fourteen years, who had no particular interests. He was a boy who accepted responsibility, and was doing well at school. S also asked about the group's activities. D said they played football and table-tennis, but otherwise got into mischief – nothing serious, but they played childish games and played jokes on people. S asked if D thought the descriptions he had given indicated what Jim might need at this stage. D said he needed friends – 'perhaps I have encouraged the responsible side of him too much; he needs to be a child sometimes'.

Comments

D's emphasis at that time was usually on helping young people to accept discipline, and to become responsible within a disciplined setting - to conform. This meant that he frequently limited his observations and actions to these aspects. In this instance he believed that Jim could be more responsible if he was helped individually and discouraged from being with his friends and getting into mischief S's questions were geared to bringing out more information about the boy and his group. She then asked D to reconsider Jim's needs in the light of the information. D saw that Jim had needs other than those he had described earlier. The techniques of drawing out more information helped workers to understand the opportunties and value of gathering as much information as possible before drawing conclusions, and sometimes helped them see which particular aspect of a situation they tended to concentrate on, and the reason for this.

EXAMPLE 4
DRAWING OUT FACTORS TO MAKE A DECISION

E's club was a central one, used by smaller clubs in the area. It was a new, purpose-built centre, and provided a setting for interesting new developments and experiments. E enjoyed his work very much, organising a staff of part-time helpers and volunteers, supported by his management committee and youth officer. He became well known in the area. He found it difficult to get involved in relationships with members with whom his contact was mainly about activities or tasks to be done. Suddenly E's club was burned down (not by a member). He came to a session a fortnight later, still in a state of shock.

E described what had happened, and said that a small, rather dilapidated building was to be used for the club. He was pleased that members' groups were meeting in houses and cafés, and said that helpers old and new were offering to help if they could. E then described the shock and his feelings, saying he still did not know what to do. E's contacts with members and helpers since the fire were discussed. S asked if maybe E felt he had lost more than the building – the members were still there, but could his status have gone with the building? E said the building was not as important as the members, but S was fairly convinced that he only partly believed this. E then said he hadn't told S the worst – that he had applied for a job in the north , the day after the fire. He said it was the only job he would have wanted – amazing that it should have turned up at that moment – that it meant his wife would not have to go on working, and he had talked it over with the youth officer, who understood his position.

At this point S realised that this seemed to be the crossroads for E. Overnight his image, which he liked, had disappeared. He was faced with a different kind of hard work, including manual work, with little to offer the members except himself. This was an opportunity to learn from his involvement with members but it seemed as though he couldn't take it. S was strongly tempted to point this out, or to urge him to stay. But she realised it was vital for E to make his own decisions.

While S was thinking out how to help E, he described again in detail his reasons for wanting the new job. S then asked E if he would have applied for the job if there had not been a fire. He said he would not have done so. She asked if he were satisfied that he would be able to help the staff and members to cope without him in their new situation. E said he thought he could do so, and described ways of helping them. But he followed this by saying, 'I am no longer sure about it. I have never faced this kind of decision before. I am in a state of indecision for the first time in my life. I applied when I was in a state of shock. But there are still many reasons why I should go.' S asked if it would help for them to list together the advantages and disadvantages of staying and leaving. E agreed.

Then followed a discussion of an hour in which a variety of factors were considered. S suggested that E's home responsibilities were important and needed to be examined. E said he did not want his wife to work – the new job would mean she need not do so. He considered alternatives if he stayed – that if he could acquire a house, this would mean no expenditure on a furnished flat, that it might be possible for his wife to work from home. S then suggested that E might list his reasons for wanting this particular job. He did so, and whereas previously he had given reasons why he should take it, he then began to list the advantages and disadvantages of the new job. This led to a consideration of future prospects, and E reflected on where he wanted to get eventually – a responsible job in the sphere of training and/or new developments. S then suggested that E should evaluate the new job and the present job, working out how each might help him reach his goal. He did so in detail.

S asked E how he felt about leaving, and how he thought other people might feel. He said he felt he was needed, but also felt that he must get away. He commented on the sympathetic way in which the youth officer had accepted his leaving, and thought other people would feel the same way. S suggested that E was now making the fire his real reason for going – did he expect people to accept that he had no choice because of the fire? E thought for a while and said he had been imagining that his interviewing committee would accept the fact that as his club was burned down he had to get a new job, that he could now see he was kidding himself. He had the choice of staying and continuing the work, and other people would know this – and now he knew it. The discussion ended with a summary of the factors considered, and E said he now needed time to think about them.

A few days later E said lie had cancelled his application. 'I must have been mad', he concluded.

Comments

In this session it was essential to draw out as many factors as possible to help E make a considered decision instead of an emotional one. The techniques used were listening to the description of the situation as understood by E, followed by tentative questioning in order to understand how E was feeling about it. When E expressed indecision, S suggested an exploration of factors and E agreed to this. Both were aware of what was happening. The technique then used was suggesting factors which could be explored – some of which had already been presented by E. The final factor was E's feelings, and in considering these E was able to realise that he had been rationalising his feelings and expecting that other people would accept his rationalisation. At this stage E wanted to think by himself, and the technique used by S was to leave the discussion without conclusions.

EXAMPLE 5
DRAWING OUT NEEDS AND WAYS OF TAKING ACTION

H was worried about the number of young people who were taking drugs, and about its possible effects. (This was some time before the problem had widespread publicity.) He had worked out his own attitudes and action in his club with regard to a group of boys who were taking drugs. They knew that he disapproved of drugs, and that if a boy produced some in the club he would be asked to leave. The boys accepted this, and as they remained in the club H was able to help them in other ways. But he was aware that they found ways of taking drugs without his knowledge. At the same time, H was usually able to isolate this group from the rest of the club, sometimes by discussing drug taking with the other members, and sometimes by standing quietly between this group and others while carrying on conversations. But this situation was a strain on H and he felt that he, and the boys, needed much more help. He had found a doctor who was helpful but busy, had read leaflets, and had discussed the subject with other youth workers.

In one session, H brought with him a collection of leaflets about drugs, and said he needed help in understanding more about it, and that he was worried. S suggested that he might consider the kinds of help he needed. H started by describing some of the difficulties he had encountered, but was not clear as to where the real problems lay. S suggested, and H agreed, that it might be useful for him to write down all he knew about drugs, and young people taking drugs. This would not only clarify his own mind, but would help him to be concise in presenting a situation.

H then said he felt that although people were concerned, it was difficult for anyone to do anything about it, and also that he felt that there was more to be understood about drug-taking and he wanted to know the kind of help he should be giving. S said she thought that he needed the help of someone who knew more about reasons for taking drugs, their effect, and the most helpful action to take, that she was not qualified to give this help, but they could consider how he could get it. H agreed. In the following discussion, H worked out three possibilities:

(a) that H would get together a group of youth workers who were concerned about the problem, so that they could share experiences and difficulties, and possibly find someone knowledgeable about drugs to arrange seminars

(b) that H would discuss the problem with sociologists and people from the medical profession

(c) that H could arrange for a period of supervision with a psychiatrist or someone who understood the problem more clearly, and that if this were decided upon, S would try to find a suitable person.

H was relieved to have found these possibilities and went away to think about them and take some action.

102

Comments

This was a situation in which H's attitude and action with regard to members had been worked out to some extent. H was worried and appeared to need at least three things – more information, the support of fellow workers, and the help of someone who knew more about reasons for taking drugs, their effect and the most helpful action to take. These three aspects came to light through a discussion, in which supervision was used merely to work out what H required and how it could be found. Three techniques were used – first, drawing out factors so that H was helped to express what he wanted and needed; second, bringing out into the open, a point of which H was aware, that the supervisor's help was limited, and he needed to look elsewhere; third, helping H to work out specific ways in which he could get help. Although this example is of a worker and a social problem, these techniques were used in other, more simple situations.

CHAPTER NINE

Skills and Techniques – using records

INTRODUCTION

ALTHOUGH the skill and techniques as described applied to all learning in supervision, whether the material used was verbal or recorded, there were particular points to be considered in helping a worker to use records. If a worker had been inarticulate, skill would have been needed in helping him to talk. When a worker could talk about his work descriptively, skill was needed to help him find other words to use in describing the work (by applying theories or introducing other factors). The same considerations were necessary when a worker wanted to, or did, write about his work instead of talking about it. The skill was in understanding what prevented a worker from writing and what was needed to help him do so, in understanding the techniques which could be used to help him become more aware of its value to his learning, and in knowing how to develop his ability to write effectively if he wished to do so.

ADMINISTRATIVE RECORDS

The first point to be considered was the necessity for using all and any records presented by the worker. The supervisor's function was not to insist on a particular way of writing, but to understand the worker's starting point in writing, and to help him build on this to increase his learning. One example of this was in starting from a worker's ability to record for administrative purposes.

A youth worker is constantly recording for administrative reasons – details of members, numbers, lists of activities, reports for committees, time schedules, minutes of meetings. Frequently these records are used to determine policy or evaluate the work, by the worker, the management committee, the youth committee or the members. If his figures show that ninety-nine per cent of the members are over seventeen years, a worker must ask numerous questions before deciding whether the club is fulfilling its most useful function in the area. If he reports that all the chairs in the club have been broken, he will presumably provide background information so that the management committee, instead of rising in wrath, will consider what action should be taken. Records of this type are used to evaluate work and determine policy, but obviously a worker is learning about some aspects of his work as he writes and uses them. It is important therefore that he should also be aware of the value of these records to his learning. If he finds it difficult to write records for the express purpose of learning, these records could be used as a bridge towards helping him to do so.

A variety of administrative records were used in the project as they were presented, with a two-fold purpose – to strengthen a worker's confidence by using material he prepared (as opposed to worrying about the mystery of recording), and to work towards a time when recording could be seen as one whole process in which there were many aspects (administration, training, interpretation, etc.).

EXAMPLES

D wanted an addition to his staff, and in supervision worked out the types of information required for a report to convince a committee. E had prepared a report for his committee which he hoped would show the need for a change of policy. He discussed the validity of the information lie had prepared, the knowledge and skills he had used in organising It into a report, and the possible reactions of committee members. J discussed the minutes of a meeting because, although he knew they had recorded decisions, he was not satisfied that they reflected the attitudes of the committee members. X, who was worried about time, presented his timetable for a week from which he was able to look at his own priorities in relation to the needs of people with whom he was working. H prepared his contribution to an annual report, and then studied this by questioning himself on what he wanted the committee and subscribers to understand about the club, and the effectiveness of the report in presenting such information.

In these and other examples, workers were using records, required in their work, mainly by other people. They learned how their range of information could be increased, so that the records could achieve their purpose more effectively. In doing this they began to understand, if they had not already done so, how written material could be explored so that more factors in the situation could be recognised.

USING DIFFERENT KINDS OF RECORDS
The starting point for workers who wanted to record their work so that they could learn more about it, was frequently a diary of events as observed by the workers. Sometimes these were brief sentences or a description of an incident. The implicit or explicit questions were:

'Could these be useful for training?' or, 'How could these be useful for learning?' In order to answer the questlons they had to be used. The following example illustrates how the shortest sentence in the project was used.

EXAMPLE I

A BRIEF COMMENT

Record (with other unrelated Sentences) by G:

'Acceptance by a new member, John – use of Christian name – must chat up.' S asked why G thought he was accepted by the new boy. G replied that when a new boy called him by his Christian name, that meant that G was accepted by him. S said it sounded as if new boys were a species. As G didn't understand this, S said, 'Do you find that all new boys are the same?' G said, 'No', so S asked what made him think that all new boys behaved in the same way in this instance. G said he hadn't thought about it, and began to think about several new boys In his club, remembering reasons why they did or did not use his Christian name. He became interested in this, describing their behaviour individually, their relations with other boys, and their attitudes to they club and himself. Then he said, 'I've been thinking about myself, haven't I? Not about the boys at all – and I had my own ideas as to what my Christian name must mean.'

...The discussion continued.

Comments

In this example the supervisor started by noting that an assumption had been made in the record. She related this to G's early concern that he jumped to conclusions without exploring the facts. This thinking produced her first question. She could have started In at least three other ways:

(a) What is important about this incident? (vague)
(b) Is acceptance by a new member important to you? (towards introspection)
(c) How was John's acceptance of you important to him? (this might have led to more information about John and his needs).

In fact, (a), (b) and (c) were touched on in the discussion, of which the record covers only a part, but starting from any point could have led to a discussion including boys and their individual needs and attitudes, relations between boys and the worker, the worker as seen by himself and boys, and the worker's feelings and awareness. The technique used here was questioning, and the skill was in knowing how to question so that many aspects of the incident were explored. Although G learned about himself in his work from a discussion of this record, it is unlikely that the session encouraged him to expand his recording. He came to another session with a similar record, but this time he was already prepared with questions about it.

EXAMPLE 2

'Usual group on second floor. Always locking pass door, don't leave key in lock – enables me to get in with my key. Who are they trying to keep out? Are they afraid they wouldn't be able to cope with trouble? Trouble from whom? Feeling of being special? Feeling of security? of being trusted?'

G started the session by saying he was interested to know why the group wanted to lock itself into a room. There was very little factual information in the record, and for a large part of the session S was drawing out information about the group, its members, its relation to the total club, etc., until eventually G saw possible reasons for their behaviour and later was able to take helpful action. At the end of this session G realised how much more information he needed before he could begin to answer his own questions, and that this information changed some of this questions. He could see now a value in recording factual information and started to do this.

Comments

The skill, techniques, and purpose in learning from this record, were similar to those in the first example, but with the added purpose of helping G to see that he could have observed and recorded factual information, together with the value of doing so.

EXAMPLE 3

G came to the third session with a tape-recording instead of written records. This appeared to be partly because he had become frustrated with the slow speed of writing factual records, and partly because he was uncertain how he could record a group session in which he was involved. He arrived with tapes of a meeting with a boys' group which was planning the re-opening of a dance club. He asked S if she would mind listening to it, and said he had not known what to look for in the session. He said the boys had not minded the recording, and after a few minutes had ignored it. S agreed to use this as recorded material.

The discussion was difficult to follow as S couldn't grasp the accent and language quickly enough, nor could she place the speakers most of the time, even though G had described the group members. it was inevitable, therefore, that S concentrated mainly on G's contributions and she noted that he seemed extremely nervous. S had not seen this in G before, and wondered if he had difficulty in relating to some of the members.

At the end S expressed her difficulties in understanding what was happening in the meeting, and G gave details to throw light on individuals and the discussion. S said that G had seemed nervous – was it the recording? G said he had been nervous, but he didn't think it was the tape, he just hadn't been sure how to handle the meeting. S suggested that they should look at where the ideas had come from – who had made suggestions, and what had happened to them. G agreed and replayed parts of the tape so that these facts were noted. S commented on a suggestion by a boy on seating accommodation and asked G what had been the boy's reaction when G had accepted his suggestion as a good one. G said, 'He was delighted and became very helpful in the discussion'. S asked G if he thought this exchange of ideas could have anything to do with relationships. G thought about this, saying slowly, 'The boy suggested something – he was giving – I accepted the suggestion – I was taking – then (relating to seminar) relationships are exchanges, giving and taking but, of course this means that when a boy suggests something I don't only think of the suggestion but of what its acceptance or rejection means to that boy.' G was very pleased with this insight and although the discussion continued he could not concentrate. S said, 'I guess you want to think about this.' G said, 'Yes, I do – it makes all the difference – maybe I'll write down some of these records and look at what happened with regard to suggestions and relationships.' He hurried away.

Comments
The difficulties of using a taped record were that so much time had to be spent in listening, and that individuals could not easily be identified. Although later, individual sessions were recorded occasionally, this method was not used again for a group. Through the use of a tape, S recognised G's hesitation in participating, and from this wondered about his relationship with those particular boys. G did not know how to use the tape for learning and therefore S suggested that they should consider the boys' contributions. When the contributions were considered factually, S questioned G about them so that he could relate his observations to a theory. In doing this, G suddenly had insight into a meaning of relationships. He could not think beyond this insight and went away to explore it more thoroughly. The techniques used by S were questioning again. The skill was in recognising G's need at that moment - to understand his relationships with boys, and to understand how to use a record - and in relating the two, so that both could be met. A second skill was in knowing how to help relate practice and theory – that is, in understanding the questions to ask so that G could do so.

EXAMPLE 4
A GROUP AND AN INCIDENT
At a time when C was not sure what she wanted to learn because she had no problems, she decided to start recording a group, mainly in order to understand how to use records. She brought the following record to her session.
'THE BANBURY GROUP
Tom 17 yrs, Alan 18 yrs, Paul 16 yrs, Chris 17 yrs, Tim 17 yrs, John 17 yrs, Dick 17 yrs, Laurie 17 yrs, and others, including Susan. All were members of the Sixty Youth Club, also of Banbury, except for Paul who is on waiting list. Left Banbury because of atmosphere – i.e. leather-jacket rockers didn't like them. Some talk of fights and threats – difficult to separate truth from fiction.

Tom assumes role of leader but questionable whether he really is all the time. Most of group like to dance together – except for Tom who scorns them for it. Appears to want (?) to look after group.

Three work on railway. John used to. Others generally involved in electrical work of some kind.'

'Incident:

Big argument between John and Laurie regarding John being unfit to drive his scooter home after a drinking session. Chris backed up Laurie. Laurie won and John left his scooter. Group generally seemed to approve of Laurie's action. Tom came in towards end of conversation but didn't join in. Later he said he often (with the others) saw various members safely home when they were drunk. Lauries was not regarded as hero – nor John especially to blame. Group accepted situation as normal.'

C said she wasn't sure if the record were useful. She had started to describe the group members and their background, then she found she couldn't go on, and she had then recorded the incident. S asked why she had recorded this particular incident. C said she wasn't sure except that she felt that there was something interesting about the group that she didn't understand. S asked C if she could develop this and C described the group's ability to make decisions, to support each other and to get along in public, even though they were dressed as mods. S asked more questions about the group which C could answer in detail, describing their family, school and work backgrounds, the things they had in common, the reason they had come to her centre, their relationship with each other, their activities. The word 'mature' appeared constantly. Eventually there was a very detailed picture of the group and its members.

S reminded C of recent seminar discussions, and asked if she could think how the factors she had described could be affecting the group. C thought for a while and then said, 'They can look after themselves. They are a self-programming group. I knew there was something I didn't understand. I felt I ought to be doing something about them because they were dressed as mods, but I didn't know what it should be.' She described the incident again, and said, 'I think I was worrying about the argument and the drunkenness. I didn't see the importance of the group members' handling their own situation. I was worried because I was doing nothing about the trouble so perhaps that is why I wrote down the incident.' S asked C if she had ideas about what the group needed in the club. C thought an adult atmosphere, facilities, a meeting place, etc., and then remembered that she had suggested a car rally to them and they had jumped at it.

C was pleased with the session and commented on how much she had learned. With a little help, C then described again why she had written the records, how they had been used, the expansion into producing many new factors about the group, followed by a greater awareness about the group and a new understanding of her original concern, and a knowledge as to how she and the club could be used by the group.

Comments

C had two particular needs. The first, of which she was unaware, was to understand how to relate different factors in group behaviour, so that they had meaning in terms of people. The second, of which she was aware, was to learn how to record and use records. S had to help C to meet the first need in order to help her meet the second. C had been dissatisfied about an incident in the club, but she couldn't think why. She had started to write about the members concerned, but this had seemed purposeless, so she had described the incident. The first technique used was questioning, so that C could recognise how much she knew about this group. The second technique was in relating the numerous factors in this group to C's theoretical knowledge about group behaviour. C then understood that in the incident she had consciously observed only certain factors – drunkenness, arguments and appearance. From these observations she was concerned about her own lack of action. She had discounted her own observations of the group members' actions in coping with their own problem.

Exploration of her knowledge of the group clarified the behaviour of the group, and also C's value judgements as opposed to her more considered judgement of the group. Once she was able to relate all her knowledge of the group, C was able to see what they needed from the club and from her. The third technique used was questioning C, drawing her out, so that she could describe what and how she had learned from her record – from the moment she had thought about recording the incident, to her final insights. She was then analysing the session itself.

EXAMPLE 5
EXPANDING INCIDENTS

At times workers recorded actual information in diary form. They needed help in expanding their records, that is, in understanding other facts which could be usefully recorded, in recognising different types of facts available, and in exploring the kinds of information required to understand behaviour, and draw considered conclusions. A wanted to learn more about group behaviour, how to observe it and analyse it. He decided to record, in diary form, the holiday when he and his wife took nine members abroad.

A Supervision Session I

A had posted his records (11 pages). S asked if A had found the records useful. A said the records had been useful as a record of camp, but he would like help in finding out their value. S wondered if A had gained any overall impression on reading the records – no, except an emphasis on eating. S said it might be interesting to find out why this emphasis. Her own impression was that the group appeared to form a series of changing sub-groups throughout the holiday, except at the end when they were in trouble – was this a fact and, if so, had it been intentional? A said he thought it probably was like that, but that he hadn't consciously tried to make anything happen – he had just observed what was happening and had written it down. S thought this doubtful, but suggested they should look at the purpose of the camp. A said it was that the members should enjoy themselves. S, 'In which eating played an important part?' A, 'Yes, it did'. Then followed a discussion on ways in which the holiday had helped the members to enjoy themselves. From this emerged three questions:

(a) How did each incident recorded help members to enjoy themselves?
(b) How did each incident help the group to become more closely knit?
(c) What part did A play in the incidents, and through this how did he help all to enjoy themselves?

A said he would use these questions on some of the incidents for his next session. S pointed out that in asking these questions there was an assumption that cohesiveness in a group was a contributory factor in enjoyment.

A Supervision Session 2
Incident – putting up tents – from original record:
'On arrival – we said it would be best to get the tents up first (we had travelled for two days and it was 9 p.m. and dark). Boys got on with theirs and Mary and I put ours up. The boys were reluctant to help the girls. John said they had been in Wales with us and knew how to put them up. Tom said he wouldn't mind helping but they hadn't started even. The girls hadn't got a clue how to start. I thought I would get on with something else and see what happened. The boys just went back to their tent and left the girls to it – by this time they had the tent out of its bag and were chatting up a few German boys to help them. Within a short while only Jane was left holding the torch for the Germans; the others had either gone to wash or were in the café. This was after they had got their cases while the Germans worked. I gave them some money to go and get some supper (we were exhausted and went to bed). Girls said they couldn't find anywhere open but the boys got a meal.'

Recorded comments on incident by A for second session:
'Boys left girls to it after some discussion, realised their difficulty but would not help. Wanted the girls to do their fair share of the work. Could be that they wanted the group to work together on all future chores, so set standard at beginning. But more likely that they felt that the girls should do their own work so did not help with the cohesion of the group. The girls got most of their enjoyment from the "chatting up" of the German boys and this gave them satisfaction in their achievement, and when this was accomplished they were off, leaving Jane to it.'

A said he realised he hadn't answered the three questions on the first incident. He provided more background to the incident and said it resulted in the group being divided. S suggested that they should start from the beginning of the incident.

What happened?
A decision was made.

Who made the decision?
I suggested it, and it was agreed the tents should go up, but there was discussion and grumbling about how it was to be done.
What did you do?
I put up my own tent following the decision. I also said ifanyone wasn't sure of points I could demonstrate with my tent. The boys used this offer, but not the girls.

A discussion followed on the boys' needs in relation to A's offer, and the girls' needs in relation to it. The boys were able to accept and use it and carry out the decision. The girls wanted to attend to their clothes and go out and were unable to accept the offer or act on the decision.

Did anyone help the girls?
No.
What about Tom?
He would have done with encouragement, but he didn't get any.
So if the girls could not keep to the decision, they would have to fend for themselves?
Yes.
What did they do?
They got help elsewhere – they found the Germans, who put their tent up.
So they didn't keep to the agreement, left the group temporarily and found help elsewhere?
Yes, the group split up.
Did the girls enjoy themselves?
Yes, they did with the Germans. The friendship lasted.
So the girls found enjoyment outside the group?
Yes, this was typical of the holiday. Many contacts were made outside the group as compared with none last year. Now I think of it, as a result of last year we had decided to encourage members to mix with other groups.
So there was another purpose in the holiday – getting to know people outside the group.
Yes, I'd forgotten about it, but that is what we wanted.
What happened to the girls later?
They couldn't find their way and came back. They felt strange and it was dark.
And the boys?
They didn't worry about them.
What about you?
I was dead tired and left them to it.
How then did you help the cohesion of the group?
I didn't – I opted out.

Two discussions followed – first on ways in which A could have helped the cohesion of the group if he had wanted to. Second, on the situation in terms of interplay between individuals, sub-groups, the whole group and contacts with other groups. A related this to his concern (discussed in earlier sessions) about the variety of groups in his club, the interaction between them, and his own role in his club.

Incident 2 – Looking for a restaurant – from original record:
'Suggested we went into B – as still raining. Spent half-hour looking for reasonable priced café for a meal without success - ended up in dear restaurant of hotel – no choice on menu under 10s. each. Girls reluctantly agreed to take a chance on what it was, but only Kate and Jane liked it. Peter did not eat any. John not much. Tom and Geoff ate most of the left-overs of the others and said that they were silly (I thought it was delicious). Geoff and Tom stole toilet rolls from the toilets (no toilet paper at the camp site). Then split up leaving the boys chatting up two girls in the hotel, though Pete was only waiting for the others.'

Recorded comments on incident by A for second session:
'All together looking for place to eat that is reasonable, all getting wet in rain rushing looking in different restaurants, and reporting back at intervals to compare prices in Austrian sch. and app. English equiv. Helped the individuals by allowing them to have status in the group because each one reported on how much, and what it was, and how they had managed to translate all these things.

The cohesion of the group was helped by all being engaged on the same thing and all wanting the same result, a good cheap meal that they could understand. It was helped also by their coming to a decision after girls had refused to take 'pot luck'.

How did I help? only by suggesting where they looked for restaurant and what to look for, etc., and helping in the final decision by saying I was willing to eat wherever they suggested.

Boys had great enjoyment in trying to speak the language to local girls and the waiter. This gave them a sense of achievement. Although not all enjoyed the meal, the group were together and acting together discussing the merits and demerits of it. Made decisions on who should steal the toilet rolls, etc. Also was instructive on how they would select future meals and how their limits of spoken and sign language would work. Group parted by mutual consent.'

S said that A's comments on the incident had brought more information into it. A said that as he had begun to write them he had recalled other factors. He then described the incident a third time, producing a vivid picture of the town square, in pouring rain, with himself in the middle under an umbrella, and group members dashing from him to suggested restaurants in and around the square, studying the menus outside amidst laughter, and rushing back to compare prices. Then a consultation in the rain, and a combined rush to the hotel restaurant. Here a drying-out, animated discussion round the table, A helping the group to come to a decision relating to prices and possibilities, continued discussion about the food, a more surreptitious discussion about the toilet rolls, and then consideration as to what this experience had taught in terms of future meals. A was able to remember comments made by members, attitudes to each other, and the part he had played.

S tried to help A to describe the situation in different ways by asking 'What was happening when . . .'. A recognised that among factors affecting the cohesion and morale of the group were the weather, that everyone had the same goal, the full participation, the subjects for discussion, the group v. the restaurant re the toilet roll, the decisions, A's own participation. When S asked why A had put in the comments that he had 'only made suggestions', he said he had not realised then that he was doing any more. He looked in detail at his participation in the group, and commented on the difference between the original few sentences and his final description. When asked if he had noticed what caused the difference, he said that the questions made him look for other factors, and he could then recall much more. The incident was seen as one which helped the cohesiveness of the group, and in which there was apparently enjoyment for everyone. It was noted that if emphasis had been on observing relationships between individuals, even more specific recording of discussion and behaviour would have been necessary.

Comments

When A recorded his camp he made certain observations and wrote them down. Although they were inevitably selected, they were not recorded with any particular purpose in mind. There were several ways in which these records could have been used for learning, and as A wanted to understand how they could be used, S chose a method of helping A to expand his own records. In discussion she asked the purpose of the situation and she helped him find his own questions to use on records. A then expanded parts of the records by applying his questions to certain incidents. On the first incident he was unable to answer the questions, so S went through the incident with him, questioning and reflecting back what was happening. In this way, more information was recalled, described and considered with different concepts. As a result, A understood his own role more clearly and was able to relate this understanding to his work with groups in his club. A was able to describe the second incident three times, each time recalling more information, so that eventually he had a clearer picture of the behaviour of the group and of his own role in it. He was then able to draw a number of conclusions about this group, the incident in relation to the purpose of the holiday, his role, and recording.

THE WORK AND/OR THE RECORD

In all these examples, which were taken from the earlier stages of the project, the supervisor was trying to do two things together – to help the workers, through the record they had presented, to understand their work and to understand the value of recording. They wanted to understand the value of recording, but they could do this only if they learned something about their work when using the record. The supervisor therefore always began with the record, however unpromising it seemed, so that the worker recognised that his effort had some point. If he knew what he wanted to learn from the record she helped him to study it to see if the information were adequate. If it were not she helped him recall more information to relate to the recorded material, until he could learn what he wanted. If the worker did not know what he wanted to learn, the supervisor took the initiative in drawing out more information to see what could be learned about the situation recorded. In all of these actions she was helping a worker to examine factors in a situation, increase the number of factors to be observed, and then to analyse them, and consider his own action as a result of the analysis.

Incidental to this, she was helping him to use a record, to understand the difference between recorded fact and opinion, to expand his records, and to learn questions to bring to bear on a record, so that he could analyse it. He was therefore learning to expand his record and analyse it, using the supervisor as questioner only until he was ready to do it for himself It was only through constant practice of preparing and using records, with the supervisor taking this role, that a worker was able to widen his range of information, from which to observe and question, and to understand how to expand and analyse records.

Sometimes workers wanted to learn how to use the records, without learning about their work through them. This meant that they learned very little – their minds were on the records while the supervisor was helping them look at the situation described. Sometimes workers wanted to analyse a situation with too little information, to write one or two sentences of fact, followed by a conclusion. Sometimes they found it interesting that one sentence from them could produce so much learning. All these and many other factors had to be considered when helping workers to learn to use their own records.

For most workers, it was only in the second year, when they were recording their own supervisory sessions, that they began to record, analyse their record, and bring their own conclusions to supervision for discussion.

CHAPTER TEN

From Supervisee to Supervisor

IT IS, not by accident that, following a detailed exploration of the factors to be acknowledged and understood in developing skill, this chapter describes how workers with no previous experience gradually developed skill in supervising – through practice, and examination of their practice. Supervising was a slow process of understanding specific incidents and behaviour, and although this meant hard work and concentration at first, like any other skill it gradually made sense, and was seen as something which could be acquired.

NEW LEADERS AND NEW SUPERVISORS

The description of supervision in this report began with a recognition of the attitudes, feelings and expectations of the people concerned. As might be expected, these were slightly different for new leaders and new supervisors, and needed special consideration.

Youth leaders came out of college and into their first jobs with mixed feelings – with a sense of achievement at having stayed the course, of relief at having completed it, of apprehension at the thought of the responsibility to be undertaken, and of anticipation that their ideas could now be put into practice. But all the careful preparation in college could not equip most of them to deal with the situation in which they found themselves, without some emotional upheaval. Areas of their work in which they felt confident were challenged not only by members, but sometimes by colleagues and management committees from whom they expected support. Two leaders had no management committees, and one of these felt responsible to three separate bodies. Other committees had no previous experience of employing full-time leaders, and were not necessarily united in their ideas of success for a club, or of efficiency in a leader. A first difficulty arose for many leaders when they attempted to carry out their own ideas for youth work, explain these to the committee, and at the same time carry out an ill-defined management policy. While this was happening, many leaders were expected, because they were trained, to be competent and produce results (not defined), possibly because of a general urgency to improve youth work. It is doubtful whether anyone stated in such terms that results were expected, but it seemed implicit in odd remarks, and leaders felt it.

At the same time, many leaders were struggling for recognition as professional leaders, when they were not sure what a professional leader should be or do. They felt they had to be successful in their probationary year, but were not sure who should be pleased in order to achieve success. All of these factors appeared to contribute to a leader's inability to go slowly, to assess what was already happening in a club, and delay innovations until he understood the immediate situation. Instead, leaders frequently made changes which they thought would be helpful, and sometimes, if these were resisted, tried to convince others and themselves that they had a particular role and knew what to do, as they were professional leaders. Some leaders did not try to convince but listened, and became frustrated or confused when they could not understand what action would be acceptable. These are some of the comments in supervision made by new leaders.

'I sometimes feel like God, and need to have my views questioned.'
'I want to establish myself as the overall leader.'
'I must do the ethical thing.'
'Some don't want to be called youth leaders, but club leaders. I want to be called a youth leader.'
'I want to let them know what my beliefs are, and what others believe.'
'You have to be fireproof in this job.'
'It worries me that I don't know what I am doing in this job.'
'I think he frightens me because he threatens my professional status.'
'I'm afraid of what people think – that they'll I think I can't cope.'

In spite of these difficulties, and sometimes with the help of a youth officer, of a chairman or of colleagues, many leaders were able to navigate and to develop work with young people in apparently active and thriving centres. Even so, most leaders accepted the offer of supervision with relief. But their expectations of help in supervision varied. Some thought their own ideas would be supported by the more experienced youth worker against the ideas of those with whom they were contending, and they were not readily prepared to accept that they themselves needed help, except in convincing other people. Some thought they would learn how a more experienced worker had coped with difficulties similar to their own. Some wanted to express their feelings about their situation, and to get some help in understanding it.

For some, being supervised added to their status, in a setting where supervision was new and not easy to find.

With this background, leaders came into supervision with feelings similar to those of anyone in a new situation, ranging through curiosity, interest, anticipation, unease and apprehension. They had already come into one problematical situation, and this new one could provide relief or could create new problems. Although their attitudes to their supervisors were similar to those of the original workers, there was a difference, because, knowing the supervisors were youth workers, they felt the supervisors must know the problems and must be able to help. Some also, for this reason, thought it would be an opportunity for open discussion – colleague to colleague – and this too affected their attitude to their supervisors. At the same time uncomfortable feelings were also present: 'Was the supervisor to be trusted?' 'Would he talk?' 'What would the project supervisor know?' It was with these and other mixed feelings, attitudes and expectations that the new leaders approached supervision.

The new supervisors were also approaching their practice with feelings of apprehension and anticipation. They wanted to supervise, to acquire new skill, and to help new leaders, but they also wondered if they were capable of doing so. They were conscious of being youth workers and some wished they had a recognised status, for they felt that not only would their youth leadership affect the attitudes of the supervisees, but they themselves would find difficulty in being both colleagues and supervisors. They wanted to take on the responsibility of supervising – it provided opportunities and/or status, but they did not want to accept the responsibility of supervising – it brought limitations to their behaviour and made them different from their colleagues.

The workers were only partly aware of these feelings before they started, but understood them more clearly during the first few weeks. At first, in their discussions, the workers emphasised how the supervisees would feel – that this was different from how they had felt when they were first supervised. Then the discussion changed, and workers commented that they must be feeling different from how the project supervisor had felt at the beginning of the project. Some of the concern about being youth workers then emerged from this discussion and was clarified.

But these feelings affected the attitudes and behaviour of workers in several different ways when they began to supervise. Although they felt they wanted to do otherwise, one worker said, 'I gave him advice – after all, I am more experienced', and another 'I visited his club. I could hardly refuse', and another 'I explained how I dealt with my situation – it was so similar to hers'. Two workers felt inhibited about the help they could give in supervision, saying, 'If only I weren't supervising I could help him, but in the setting of supervision I am not myself.' Sometimes workers tended to identify with supervisees' attitudes to authority or to the variety of expectations, or on the other hand to emphasise the points of view of the other adults concerned.

Although the feelings affected the workers' attitudes and behaviour when supervising, their earlier experience helped them to become aware of the feelings and their effect, and to understand and accept this – an important factor – for it was in understanding and handling their own feelings and difficulties, and in understanding those of the supervisee, that the worker was able to establish a relationship in which the supervisee could learn.

EARLY DIFFICULTIES IN SUPERVISING

Weaknesses return

The workers' first difficulties appeared to be that in moving into a new situation, weaknesses with which they had learned to deal in their ongoing work reappeared. Workers who had found it hard to take the initiative earlier, could not do so again. Some, who had to show their knowledge, gave advice or explained problems. Some, who had been confused, became confused again, and some who had made value judgements returned to this. But this time it was the workers who quickly recognised what they were doing and why they were doing it, and with a little help they were able to understand, deal with and in most instances change their behaviour.

How does one respond?

A first question was 'How do I know when to speak?' When supervising, a worker found it easy to listen, and was genuinely interested in the situations described, so he asked for more information. But he quickly realised that something had to be done with the information, that this was no ordinary conversation, that there were many factors on being confronted by a supervisee which he had not considered before. So he wondered how to interrupt, and when and why to interrupt. As there was no set answer he had to work this out in his own supervision.

A situation which arose frequently was one in which the supervisee described several incidents which appeared to please him. If the worker asked questions about the incidents, the supervisee was prepared to elaborate, but not to examine the incidents. Then a few minutes before the end of the session he would bring up a problem that was worrying him. The worker, who was ,anxious to be helpful, found that he was not able to help the supervisee to learn from the 'pleasant' incidents as the supervisee couldn't concentrate on them, nor could he be very helpful about the problem for lack of time. One worker tended to dismiss the 'pleasant' incidents, waiting impatiently for the supervisee to get to a problem so that he could be helpful. Another struggled to help the supervisee analyse the incident, and found it frustrating when the supervisee did not co-operate. Such was their initial anxiety that workers found it difficult to ask direct questions as to what the supervisee wanted to discuss, nor did they feel sufficiently confident to help a supervisee to see what was happening in the sessions. In his own supervision, therefore, a worker was helped first to see where his own responses had been helpful or unhelpful; second, to observe the patterns of presentation by the supervisee and consider reasons for this pattern; third, to work out alternative ways of responding to the presentation; and fourth, to consider how his own anxieties were affecting his actions.

How does one deal with emotion?
A second difficulty arose when at times a worker had to listen to an emotional outpouring – usually of anger directed at one or more adults, or distressed confusion because of the complexity of a situation. Normally the worker recognised that on such occasions a supervisee was incapable of thinking clearly, but the worker did not know how to handle the outburst, and was emotional when he described it in his own supervision, sometimes to the extent of having forgotten his own responses to it. One worker remembered that he had tried to change the subject, another that he had tried to get the supervisee to consider why he was feeling so strongly, '. . . but we got into an emotional bog'. In his supervision, the worker was helped to go back over the event, and to reflect on how he and the supervisee had been feeling, with possible reasons for it. In doing this, the worker was exploring what had happened in his supervising, and he himself became less worried and less agitated as he did so. Sometimes a worker could then see that after waiting until the end of an outburst, and accepting that the supervisee was feeling strongly, a slow recap of the situation might help the supervisee to think about it, instead of only being able to express feelings about it. Workers knew that responding to emotion with reassurance or a suggestion that the supervisee shouldn't worry was no help, but that they needed to understand more about it before they

could help. Once they recognised this and some of their own feelings about it, they became more relaxed when confronted with emotion.

How does one not give advice?

A difficulty for some workers was finding alternatives to giving advice. The lack of advice in their own supervision had been noted at an early stage, and they also knew that on the few occasions when they had been given advice they had either acted on it because they already intended to take the action, or they had ignored it. So, while recognising that they didn't want to give it because of its futility, they found themselves constantly doing so at first. Being youth workers, they could frequently understand a supervisee's difficulty before he did, or could see a simple way out for him. So they suggested what the supervisee should do. Also the supervisee wanted the advice of an experienced worker, and asked for it. 'They are such minor things' said one worker after telling a supervisee how to report to his management committee. 'I'll help him think for himself later.' Another worker emphasised the need to give his supervisee 'hints and tips'. Then later he said, 'I find that all I can do is give hints and tips'.

The worker needed to understand the difference between answering a need for practical information (that hardboard could be useful round the dartboard), and replacing learning with answers. Also, the worker became more relaxed when he realised that, in giving advice because he could think of nothing else to do, he was not harming the supervisee even though he was not helping him – as long as the worker didn't expect his advice to be followed. He then learned, incident by incident, to understand the help a supervisee was needing, as compared with the help he was getting. This difficulty of advice giving, like all the others, was overcome partially when the worker was able to concentrate on the supervisee instead of on himself, and was thus able to concentrate his thinking on the supervisee's needs instead of his own need to be a good supervisor. He had to come full circle from saying, 'It is good to have to do one's own thinking' (being supervised), to 'How do you help someone to think for himself?' (on first supervising), to 'I helped X to think for himself in that session' (on understanding supervising)

How does one deal with misinterpretation?

It was difficult in the early days for the workers to respond as they believed they should, in the face of great pressure to respond differently. Advice giving was one example of this, but there were others. Frequent questions from a supervisee were, 'Do you do this in your club?' 'Do you get on with your youth officer?' (or colleagues?) It was some time before workers could be sufficiently confident to explain that it was the supervisees' situations which it was important to discuss, and not their own. A similar difficulty was in responding to a supervisee's desire for an opinion, even when the supervisee had made only a comment. For example, when a supervisee commented, 'I think it is important for young people to join in activities', and was given no opinion in return, it was disconcerting for the worker later to hear the supervisee say, 'I know you don't agree with activities'. Again, when a supervisee described his difficulties with the neighbours and the worker asked questions about the neighbours – why they acted as they did, how they felt, etc. – the supervisee immediately thought that the worker was criticising him and siding with the neighbours.

To be misunderstood in this way was frustrating to the workers, but sometimes they also wondered about their own behaviour – perhaps they had disapproved of a particular attitude to activities, or had wanted the supervisee to understand other people's points of view, and perhaps they had shown this. They were confronted therefore with two problems – first, how to hold out and remain calm under pressure, and second, how to be sure they were helping a supervisee according to his own need, and not trying subtly to direct him – and they could understand this more clearly only through constant examination of what had happened in specific instances, and the reasons for it.

What does one do to a person?
Inevitably, difficulties of this kind led to workers wondering what they were doing to supervisees, and to recognition of their fear of what they might do to them. One worker said, 'He would never have thought the girl could be lying if I hadn't asked the question. Is it fair to put ideas into his head?' At first workers had seen their supervising as a response to a supervisee's need to learn; now they realised that they could not be passive in this, that they had to participate, and that whatever they said and did (and sometimes did not say or do) would have some effect or influence on the supervisee. This realisation brought with it self-consciousness, anxiety, and also a renewed sense of responsibility. All that could be done at that stage was to help workers to accept and understand these feelings, and then to reflect on what had happened In sessions so that they concentrated on specific instances, and developed skill, and confidence in that skill.

A recorded session

Before this chapter moves on to consider how workers developed skill in supervising, it might be helpful to present the following record which was of a worker's second session in supervising. This worker had the same kinds of difficulties as others. She wondered what questions to ask, and how to respond helpfully to the comments and descriptions presented. But these difficulties were left for her own thinking and supervision. While the record of this session gives an impression of the worker's feeling for what was being said and searching for helpful questions, it also indicates how the supervisee was being helped to expand her thinking, and to consider her problems. In an apparently relaxed atmosphere the foundation was being laid for much more help and learning in the future.

RECORD OF Y'S (THE WORKER'S) SECOND SESSION WITH X

'X said she had had some bother at Senior Club – someone turned off lights last night almost at 10 o'clock. She said the trouble was now that she didn't quite know how to deal with it – she felt that she just couldn't ignore it – had to let them know she wasn't going to stand this – but didn't really want to lecture them. I asked her if she thought these were the only lines open to her – to lecture or ignore. She thought and then said she supposed she could just quietly speak to each group, or she could get one of the most influential of each group to come together with her and talk about it. I asked her how she would approach them. She said if she had them all together she would have to lecture them and she could see problems in this: (a) she might not be able to get them together, and (b) they might not listen if she did get them all together. If she talked to them in groups she'd tell them how dangerous something like that might have been and try to get them to see how silly jokes can have repercussions. If she took them one from each group she'd probably try the same tactic. I asked her what she thought the effect on the members would be. She said if she lectured them she thought it might then become the thing to do to turn off the lights if they wanted to annoy her. She said she didn't think it had been planned – she'd forgotten to check that passage door was locked and obviously someone had realised that it was open – wandered through passage and then found lights box and switched them off as a joke. This was why she didn't think it would be good to lecture them. Said if she separated one from each group it could have disastrous results if she wasn't very careful – could be difficult because she might make the rest of the group resentful. She might call them together as a temporary committee and bring this up as just one of a number of things. Thought maybe if she had time she could do this. Said she would like to get a committee together but said she tended not to do things if, in fact, there wasn't almost certainty that it would be a success. I didn't say anything. She then said, "This is something I have to watch". I said, "If you know you do this, then it is something which you can recognise and look at".

123

She then said she was having to look at the joint holiday idea. She had several people from both clubs (D and A) interested. She said she could foresee problems – I asked "What kind?" She said that she thought the difference in standards of behaviour were what she thought would be most obvious. I asked in what way – she said she thought the A group would have different standards and for the good of the holiday as a, whole she would have to uphold the higher standards of the D group. I asked her why she would feel she must do this. She said because she felt that this would be necessary for the good of the holiday as a whole. I asked her how she thought this would work out. She said that the D group would be able to meet the A group and see the kind of members they might have if they expanded. The A group would have a chance to live up to higher standards. I asked her what she thought this might mean to them – she said, maybe the D group would see this as her aligning herself with them. The A group might see her in this way too and play up more if they thought she was taking sides. She said she was maybe taking the view of the D group because these were nearer to her personal standards. I asked her how she thought the two groups differed. Eventually, she said maybe the standards weren't so different on things that might matter because they all came from the same kind of area – maybe they were more superficial differences of education than standards of behaviour. Said maybe she'd have to get to know them better before she could really tell what the differences were. I asked her what she thought they might have in common on the holiday. She said she thought the holiday itself – they were all keen on camping or adventurous type of holiday. She said she wanted to get them together as a group at her home so that they could work out the details as a group rather than as two separate groups from two clubs. Said she didn't know when she could do this, though, as she would have to have some free time occasionally. Said she'd taken a night or two off from D, but didn't feel it was fair to do this. Said she couldn't take a night off from A as she didn't have enough help – silence – she said, "I don't seem able to get helpers" – I asked her if she had any local training colleges which might help – she said No, and she was getting so tired that she didn't quite know where to start and the less help she had the more tired she got and the less she seemed to be able to do anything about starting to look for helpers. I suggested that she might contact the London branch of IVS who might know of people in her area who could help, or might find someone to help even if only on a short time basis until she had more contacts. Also had she contacted the London Union who might know of possible sources of help in her area. She said she would particularly like to get in some older people, especially older men. (I get a strong hunch – coming through in various ways – that she is very conscious of being near the age of the members and is afraid of not being able to control them because of this.)'

DEVELOPING AND TEACHING SKILLS

Perhaps the hardest part of these early days for the workers was in not knowing whether they were being helpful. Supervisees were asking the workers, 'Is this what you are wanting in supervision?' and workers were reflecting it back, asking 'Was the discussion helpful to you?' It was a period of adjustment in which workers (without always knowing it) were frequently and spontaneously asking helpful questions and bringing in new factors to consider. But the supervisees were mainly wanting support at that stage, while workers were anxious to train them and to know they were doing so. The workers felt unable to evaluate their supervising, and as the supervisees could not evaluate either, some workers turned to the project supervisor for evaluation. Sometimes a worker presented a record of a session (as in first days of supervision) wanting constructive criticisms of his actions. Sometimes a worker presented a record, consisting almost entirely of a description of the supervisee and his work and comments. The worker appeared to want the project supervisor to take over the supervision of the supervisee through him.

The project supervisor's temptation was similar to that of the supervising youth worker – to pass on her own skill by demonstrating, advising, or explaining what she would have done in the circumstances. Remembering that skill is 'knowing how to' ... it is debatable whether she would have passed on more than techniques in this way, which would have been a poor substitute for understanding how to supervise. She had to rethink this therefore in terms of 'helping workers to acquire skill in supervising'. The method then became clear, though it meant moving very slowly as there was so much to understand. She had to help the worker to observe, hear, recognise and understand the needs of his supervisee – no easy task when a supervisee was unable or unwilling to express his needs; to reflect on the techniques he used in helping the supervisee to understand the material he brought; to consider his own role, behaviour and difficulties in the relationship; to relate these to the purpose of supervision. Only if a worker were able to understand and relate all these aspects for himself would he be able to develop his own skill in supervising. Obviously this method of working was fundamental to supervision, but it has been re-emphasised here because the supervisor had to understand it afresh, in new circumstances – where short cuts would have been so much easier. Equally obvious, the project supervisor's situation in helping supervisors was very similar to that of the youth workers helping youth workers.

UNDERSTANDING THE NEEDS OF A SUPERVISEE

Workers were able to recognise some needs of supervisees very quickly. In the first sessions, following descriptions of supervisees and their jobs, such comments were made as, 'He seems to be running a lively club, but I don't think he is able to look at what he is doing'. 'I think he is angry about some things, but he hides it. I should think he doesn't find it easy to express his feelings.' 'He has two clubs, no management committee, and several bodies who have different expectations of his work. He doesn't know where his loyalties lie, and I think he needs help in sorting out these groups.' 'He seems mixed up – doesn't know whether he wants to be "permissive or to educate".' These were comments about different supervisees, to which workers were able to add as they had more sessions with supervisees.

But frequently, when workers became more concerned with what they were doing than with what the supervisees were saying, learning to understand the needs of the supervisee became more difficult. The workers then missed the supervisees' needs because of their own anxiety to be helpful. Normally this was picked up in supervision with questions such as, 'How did he say this?' 'What was he really saying?' and workers developed understanding of the supervisees along with other learning in a session. But the following are illustrations of how this could sometimes be considered. All illustrations in this section describe the project supervisor as S, the worker/supervisor as Y, and the leader/supervisee as X.

EXAMPLE 1

Brief summary of extracts from Y's session with X. 'When X arrived, the new supervisee had not left, and X said he wanted a firm time for starting (though he had arrived early). Later he discussed his relationship with his youth officer, said the Y.O. never came near the club, left him to get on with his job, and was not prepared to carry the can. He finished, "He can't see where I need help." Y helped X look at ways in which he could co-operate with the youth officer and get him to provide some of the facilities he needed.'

Extract from Y's session with S. 'Y said he was not happy about that part of the session. "I helped X but not as well as I might have done and I don t know why." S suggested that they might look at X's situation as X understood it. On doing this, Y said X was obviously unsure of himself – he was worried about whether he had passed his probationary year, his management committee was reduced to three members who were not being helpful, his youth officer didn't come near, and although this might be because he thought X was competent, X saw it as disinterest - In fact, X was feeling isolated, unappreciated and worried about his work, and his comments on his arrival were connected wIth this. Y continued, "He has no one to pat him on the back occasionally". S asked what this understanding of X meant to him. Y said, "He is worried about his work and I spent no time at all on this. I helped him to look at action he could take, but ignored his feelings and worry because I didn't notice them."

EXAMPLE 2

Extract from Y's session with S. 'Y said that X had described an evening which he had spent with a group, but had not been prepared to look at what had happened, although he insisted on finishing the story of the evening before going on to a problem. S asked what he thought X wanted to say about the evening. Y thought that in the light of X's earlier difficulties, he wanted to show his ability to accept the behaviour and deal with it helpfully. S said that if that were his reason, was there any reason why X shouldn't tell the whole story? "No," said Y, "except for my anxiety - none".'

In helping a worker to recognise needs, it was essential that the supervisor should keep some balance in the early days between this and helping him meet his own needs. A worker wanted help and he had difficulties, and there were occasions where pointing out the supervisee's needs was unhelpful to the worker. The supervisor saw that her own attitude was important. If, by her behaviour, she indicated that she was saying, 'These are the supervisee's needs which you should meet' she could expect that the worker might be reluctant to discuss it, but if, by her behaviour, she was saying, 'You obviously want to understand why this didn't help, so let's look at what this supervisee is asking for', there was co-operation, because she was at the same time meeting the worker's need. In the first she was going on to the side of the supervisee. In the second, she was working with the worker who was helping the supervisee.

As the workers continued to supervise, so they tended to think more about the supervisee, and considered the help the supervisee had wanted, the help they had given, and where possible the use the supervisee had made of it. Y commented that for the first time X had continued a discussion in a second session. He thought X was progressing in some ways. S asked what made Y think this. Y said that X seemed to be more positive in the way she worked - she was thinking about sessions in between and taking action on this. S said it seemed that leaving a person 'high and dry', which he was worried about having done in X's last session, could have helpful results as well as unfortunate ones. Y agreed, and said there was a difference in the way X was looking at things. At first she had wanted 'to set all the centre right'. Now she saw that was impossible and was prepared to concentrate on what she could do.

The following is a worker's record after supervising for some weeks. In this Y was helping X to explore a situation, and while doing so was identifying the problem. By this time he was no longer depending on his own supervision for working out the needs of his supervisee.

RECORD OF Y'S SESSION WITH X

'X said he had a difficult problem in that some of his members were singing at the Club Xmas show and they had chosen to sing a very crude song. He said he did not like it but the members were determined to sing it. No song, no show! They had the club behind them as the members liked it. They had been willing to sing songs in church and hospital to please the establishment and they now wanted to sing their own song. X was worried about it because:

(a) He did not want to ban it and cause the show to fold up
(b) He did not want to allow it because of possible repercussions
(c) He felt they were pressing on with it to get one over on him
(d) He saw no way out that would suit everybody

We looked at the problem again in detail, stage by stage, bringing out new factors and thinking aloud on each new facet of the problem. X was obviously very worried about it and said he had lost a night's sleep over it. His friend had heard the song and told him to let them sing it and stop worrying. Comment: This was the only subject presented; nothing else was mentioned or discussed during the 1¾ hour session. What was he worried about? I suggested we should look at this, and we did so.

(a) That they wouldn't agree with him
(b) He did not want the ultimate authority
(c) They were trying him out
(d) It could almost cost him his job
(e) That he was being too narrow-minded. (His friend possibly thought so, but I didn't after hearing some of words in song)
(f) That they were just having a game with him and did not really expect him to allow them to sing such a song in public (to church audience)
(g) Whatever decision was made he would lose face with either the members or the church

X stated the above not as questions but more as facts, punctuated by, "Well, what would you do?" but I would not answer this nor imply.

We discussed the action he could take.

(a) Sing it to the minister and see what he thought. It would then be the minister's decision and the responsibility would be off X. X could then say the minister had decided you cannot sing it, please don't let me down about the show, etc.

(b) He could talk it over with the management committee members in terms of "This is something I am worried about, what do you think?"

(c) He could try and think up attractive alternatives for them to sing, that were not so crude but still amusing. Specific ones were mentioned

(d) It might even be possible to see if the group would look at it again and see what position they, X, the church and the club would be in if a member of the audience was shocked by the song and summoned them for obscenity, etc. Did they as entertainers come under the jurisdiction of the Lord Chancellor? Get them to look at their true motives for wanting to sing it.

No decision was reached. X said he wanted to think about these possibilities. The problem seems to be that X does not want to make a decision for himself I think he was beginning to see this, and that he doesn't want to carry the responsibility for making such a decision. We looked at this a little but perhaps later it will be possible to discuss some of his difficulties in making decisions.'

UNDERSTANDING ONE'S OWN BEHAVIOUR WHEN SUPERVISING

As in other areas where learning was from the situation, workers continued to learn about their own behaviour when learning about supervising. Again, insights of this kind were frequently small ones in passing, but on occasions they required more discussion. The following are two examples of workers considering their own behaviour as supervisors.

EXAMPLE 1

RECORD OF S's SESSION WITH Y

Y said he had made no records during the three weeks that S had been away. He said this seemed to show that he needed an outside discipline to make him record, and he wondered if this meant that an ordinary worker couldn't supervise. He had a feeling that other workers were the same and were also wondering about this. S asked if he had evidence or was guessing. Y – 'Guessing, I don't really know'. S said, 'So we are really talking about you'. Y, 'Yes, I know I need an outside discipline – though strangely enough in recent weeks, all I have done in supervision is give hints and tips. That seemed to be what was wanted. X used them as well. (Description of difficulty with management committee member.) He came back next week and told me what had happened.' S asked if Y thought there was any relation between his need for outside discipline and his own behaviour as supervisor. Y, 'Well, I am giving him my knowledge - that's what he seems to want'. S, 'What happens if you are not there?' Y. 'Yes, of course, I am not helping him think for himself. When I think of it, I don't know if hints and tips are right for the present, or if it is lack of thinking and recording that has prevented me from seeing other possibilities.' Y smiled, recognising his answer as he said this, then said, 'But he is not presenting any subtleties in supervision'. S asked what he meant. Y became confused and said finally, 'If he talked about a group of senior members and his relations with them I could help him'. S said the incident with the management committee member sounded very similar to that type of situation. Y agreed and said, 'Yes, I think I am just confused about it all, and guessing'. S agreed and suggested that without specific material to study, presumably it had to be guesswork, and guessing seemed to leave him wondering and worrying as to whether he could supervise. Y said this was true, and he knew it was from his own impatience to get results, and that he did need help in making himself record in order to understand what was happening. S suggested that if at present the help he needed to make him record was knowing that he had a supervision session coming, that was what he now had. Y smiled and said, 'Yes, I am making you my discipline whether you like it or not, and I can see that at present I am being X's discipline'.

EXAMPLE 2

RECORD OF S'S SESSION WITH Y

Y described his recorded session with X in which X had been particularly concerned about the expectations of his youth officer. Then he said, 'You know, I found this very difficult to describe. It wasn't difficult at the time, but it was difficult to describe it to you.' S asked if Y knew why, and he said, 'I was too pressing too soon and I suppose I didn't like telling you, as supervisor, what I'd done. It was muddled.' S asked Y if he had noted where the muddle was – 'No'. S asked who Y had been helping in the session. He said that he had thought he was helping X, but in looking at it he realised he had spent a lot of time pointing out the needs of the youth officer. He said, 'This is where I got carried away and went round in circles. I took him on a conducted tour of the problems.' S asked where he might have broken the circle. ' Well, I think I did the same again (earlier session) and didn't look at X and his problem. I know I shouldn't have said to him at this stage "but aren't you sensitive too" – I stuck the knife in, and he was embarrassed to no purpose.' A discussion followed about the results on a person of having a knife in him, reasons for using a knife, the knowledge of a surgeon before using a knife, and the point at which a surgeon uses a knife. Y said, 'Surgeons don't operate for fun'. S asked why Y had done this. He said, 'I know it is something in me'. S said it might be helpful to look at when Y behaved in this way. Y said, 'I go too fast. But it is more than that. It is an attack but it is also a form of defence. It is a difficulty in making a relationship – feeling one is not going to get to know what something is about, so one starts fencing.' S asked when Y did this. He said, 'It is in a new situation – when I haven't confidence in what I am doing'. S asked if Y had noticed a difference in his two supervisees. 'Well, with the first I attacked and then when I realised what I was doing I said very little for a time, and he did all the talking. Then I found I knew ways of helping him and didn't need to attack.' 'What about the second?' 'This is only the second week – but I already realise what I have done – so I won't again.' S suggested this showed that Y was more quickly aware in a new situation of what he was doing. Y agreed and said it was also making a difference in the way he thought about training groups. 'I used to make them jump, but I don't need to do that now.'

ACQUIRING AND UNDERSTANDING TECHNIQUES

Techniques have been seen as ways of communicating with a supervisee in order to help him understand and learn about himself in his work. Workers were therefore using techniques from the moment they started to supervise. But in order to develop skill in supervising, they needed to be aware of the techniques they were using, acquire new ones, and understand how and when different techniques were most appropriate. Normally the word technique was never used in supervision – it was usually a question of considering the help a supervisee required and the help that was given or not given. But sometimes techniques were pin-pointed, sometimes they were taught, and sometimes they were discussed in general terms. The four following examples illustrate different ways of thinking about techniques. The first is an illustration of a worker recognising the techniques he has used. In the second a worker is helped to understand a technique. The third is an illustration of a worker being taught a technique. In the fourth example, the worker structures the sessions and uses a number of different techniques, but within this he looks at different factors again and learns more about his own role as supervisor.

EXAMPLE 1

RECOGNISING THE TECHNIQUES USED

Y described the first session with X. He said that X had begun by saying he understood that a supervisor was non-committal and left a supervisee to draw his own conclusions but he (X) did not want that. S asked Y how he had replied and he said he had been non-committal. X had continued by insisting that as a youth leader he had to advise members, and had given illustrations of this. Y had recognised that X felt he ought to advise but then said, 'You had considered a number of factors before deciding on the advice you would give, but you didn't give the members the opportunity to study these factors for themselves.' X hadn't replied.

Y then said to S that he thought X probably liked a good argument. X had described arguments he had with his treasurer, and had indicated that he was worried about that relationship. Y had asked how these arguments affected finance – could he get the money he needed? Was his salary paid? Were there any financial difficulties or arguments? X had said there were no difficulties of this kind, and Y had commented that apparently the argument had not affected the working relationship. X had been interested to consider this. S said it seemed that Y had approached the problem from 'work' and had found a way that wasn't argument and wasn't non-committal, but a way of helping X constructively. Y agreed, but said it was sometimes difficult to hold back.

Comment

In this session with X, Y had reacted in three different ways. In the first incident he did not commit himself when X wanted an argument about committing himself In the second, when X was presenting arguments on the need to advise, Y simply pointed out a factor that X had not considered. In the third, Y was implying that arguments were not necessarily 'bad' but that one

way of evaluating them was in considering whether they were affecting the job
to be done. The need to argue might well arise again, but in his first session Y
had found techniques which prevented an argument and which at the same
time helped X to consider other factors outside himself.

EXAMPLE 2
UNDERSTANDING A SIMPLE TECHNIQUE
Y said she had left her records behind, but she described the session in which
X had spent much of the time criticising the management committee and the
leader in charge.

Y I find it very difficult to know how to handle these criticisms.
S What do you think X is doing when he criticises in this way?
Y (after time) I suppose he is judging them – giving his opinions.
S Can you think of a way of finding out where the opinions come from?
Y No, I can't think.
S if X told you he had had a good evening in the club, what would you want
  to know?
Y I should want to know what had happened to make it good. Yes, I need to
  find out what actually happened to make it bad. (Illustrations were then
  taken from material of earlier sessions, and discussed.)
Y Yes, I can't help X to understand his committee if he gives only opinions.
  All I can do is agree or disagree, so I need facts – I must help X to see this.
S And if X's opinions can't be substantiated?
Y I don't know - well, I guess he must be feeling strongly about something to
  criticise in that way. I'll have to think about this.
S Maybe our earlier recording will indicate reasons for these feelings.

Comments
Y was confused because she could not find a way to get beyond X's
opinions. She knew the difference between fact and opinions, but when
confronted in a session with these criticisms, she became caught up in some of
the feelings behind them, and could not relate her knowledge to it. It was a
simple exercise at this stage to help Y see what was happening, to relate different
situations, the 'good' one and the 'bad' one, and to understand that the same
technique could apply.

EXAMPLE 3
TEACHING A TECHNIQUE
Y brought a record of her session with X, saying she found it extremely
difficult to develop a discussion on the subject X presented. The record was
explored in order to find out what had happened in the session, and Y then said
she thought that she was not giving X a lead. She wanted to help X to think,
but was leaving him to do this on his own, and was not able to pick up the
points he made. S suggested that they should study as an exercise how the

subject presented, 'volunteers leaving', could be explored. This was then done, at first with role playing – S becoming the supervisee.

It was then agreed that in order to explore the problem, facts were needed. What facts? The number of helpers. If Y wasn't sure of the validity of the number how could she check? By getting names. Then as Y worked out questions she realised she wanted to know the number and names of those who had left, what they had done in the club, what had happened on their last night, how each one got on with adults, with members, etc. A series of questions came to light. S asked Y what she would do with the information she received. At first Y thought she would ask X what he was going to do about the volunteers who had left, but when S suggested she might go more slowly, Y thought she would summarise the facts about each helper. Ways of rephrasing the facts were considered, leading to a form of analysis. Y then decided that in drawing conclusions from the facts, X might be able to make his own decisions on the actions to take. S suggested that Y should now go through the steps she had taken, and with descriptions, Y went through Facts, Summary, Analysis, Conclusions, Action.

Y was pleased with the exercise and considered how it could be used with other subjects. S asked what Y thought she had to do in developing this method of teaching. She said she realised that she had to understand the areas of knowledge useful in considering a problem, but that from this knowledge she had to find questions, not answers nor examples. If the questions were relevant, X could provide the answers from his knowledge. She also had to be specific in the questions so that X was helped to give information. Y said she would use this method the following week as X had said he wanted to understand the volunteer problem.

Y spent some time preparing for the next session with X and then used the method with him. She told him she had been doing homework and asked lf he would agree to look at the facts. She said in her own supervision that, having been prepared, she was able to bring the discussion back to the subject when X wandered, and to keep to the point without upsetting him. Also, because of the questions she had asked, X had realised and commented that he knew much more than he thought. He was pleased with the result and knew what he was going to do about at least one volunteer.

Comments

Y was finding difficulty in helping X. She had not the tools to use, and X tended to move from one topic to another. This resulted in the two moving round in circles. At this stage S believed that structuring the session might be of use to both, and if it didn't work out it was unlikely that harm would have been done. She therefore set out to help Y acquire a technique in working with X. She went through the same exercise with Y that Y would go through with X, that of helping Y to produce the information required, to examine what it meant and what should be done with it, and to draw conclusions about it. Y not only thought through this method in relation to X, but, because she understood a way in which she could help him, she was relaxed at the beginning of the next session with him, which presumably made her help more effective. This way of teaching a technique was not used very often, but there were times, when a worker felt he had understood a supervisee's needs and couldn't help him, that such teaching gave him the confidence he required to take the initiative.

EXAMPLE 4
STRUCTURING SESSIONS AND USING DIFFERENT TECHNIQUES

In one session, Y discussed with S his difficulties in helping X. These appeared to arise because each time he tried to help X in one area of his work X indicated that nothing could be done about it because of difficulties in other areas. In particular, X was worried about not spending enough time at home, but gave many reasons why he couldn't do so. Y thought that the use of time was X's main difficulty but he could not think how to tackle it. Y and S then considered the different areas of X's work – home, administration, counselling, club programme, contact with other adults, etc. S asked Y if he thought it might be useful to structure the sessions by asking X if he would like to look at each area in terms of time. Y thought it a good idea and said he would think through it.

Y and X then structured the sessions in this way, and each week X produced a diary of how he spent his time in the mornings. Discussions arose from each item. For example, when Y commented on four hours for posters, X said they took time. Y asked if there were alternative ways of getting posters, and X commented, 'Leaders tell me I do too much'. 'Do you ?' 'Yes, but others don't do posters well enough.' This led to a discussion on values – X's idea of work and priorities, members' ideas of priorities, perfection versus participation, etc. From these discussions based on time many aspects of X's work were gradually examined. Some weeks later Y came for a session with S from which the following are extracts.

In the first part of the session, Y described a discussion with X. X had produced a plan with which he was pleased. Y said he had pointed out to X that the plan was not solving his problem. X had defended his plan and then had accepted Y's point. When telling S about this discussion, Y pointed out two ways in which the plan had been valuable. S asked Y if he had discussed with X the ways in which it was valuable. Y said he had not thought of doing so. S asked if Y understood why she had asked that question. Y thought for a minute and then said, 'Yes, I understand. My mind leaped ahead when he told me about the plan and I immediately understood what was missing in it. If I had started with him at the points at which he felt it was valuable, he could have worked out for himself what was missing.' He then said, 'I helped X, but he could have learned more himself about this'.

Then Y thought for a minute and said, 'I can see there might be times when it is useful to jump in and point out the other side of a problem, but I did this only because I thought of it and wanted to say it. One needs to be conscious of it – to be able to make the choice, knowing why. I was spontaneous but not conscious.' S said, 'Aren't the recording and your sessions here the places where you learn to become "conscious"?' Y agreed and said, 'You know – it's like the A.A. man who is coming to the club. He asked if he was to lecture and I said, "No, it needs to be quite casual." He replied, "I'll need to think about that. A casual approach needs a lot of thinking about." ' As S nodded, Y went on 'It reminds me of my last job (window-dressing). When I went from one job where my work had been very formal, I was amazed to find that the boss would throw a piece of material down casually – and it was perfect – all its lights showed. At first I didn't understand this, and I was critical. I was angry as well, because he would sweep all my formal arguments away and get mad with me. But when I saw what he meant, I practised and in time I could be casual too.' S said, 'Are there other ways of helping people to be casual, apart from sweeping away these efforts?' 'Yes, I think so – but this man was Italian and excitable.' S asked, 'Isn't this something to do with a "mystique"?' Someone appears to have a gift, to be able to do something, and then as one practises, one begins to understand what is involved in it. Then one finds there is no mystique.' Y said, 'Yes, of course, that is what is happening here. The trouble is I'm one week behind. Once I was many weeks behind, now just one week.' S asked, 'Will the situation be the same next week?' Y replied, 'No it won't - still, I shall know to stop when I think ahead, and listen to him – forward and back, that is how one must think'. S said, 'Could we put it another way? That each week, through thinking, recording and supervision, you are acquiring new factors to draw from.' Y said, 'Yes, that's it. In a session I have more things up my sleeve to use when necessary. I have to use ways of helping him to see the missing area. He must do his own thinking. He did some, but it could have been better.'

Y went on to say that X had said he was going to a course on Thursday evenings. N would look after the club (see earlier record). X had told N he would ask the seniors to help her. She had been pleased. In answer to Y, X had said he'd asked the seniors and they were going to help. (Brief discussion re X and N, and Y's hopes about X helping N.) Y had seen football in the diary and asked what it meant. X had described an incident where he had helped the team to cope with their own problem about a coach. He had also related that he had asked a girl (who agreed) if her mother would help in the canteen. Y had said, 'So now you will have another staff member'.

Y said he had then suggested they might summarise the session (see last record). X agreed and Y said he hadn't known where to start, so he asked X if he would like to. X had swallowed hard and said, 'Well, there is need to sort my time out'. Y said then he came to the rescue and pointed out things discussed.

His action to enable him to spend more time at home
Programme
Spontaneous activities
Relations between staff and ways of helping staff

Need for more staff
Football course
Help for N
Resolved football problem
Girl and mother

Y had also related this to what X seemed to have done in his work. X had been pleased and said, 'Have we really done all this?' Y had said, 'Yes, and you had a weekend off, too'. Y had then said, 'We seem to be getting some structure into this session, and if you agree we'll pick up from here next week unless there is a burning issue. This might help us both to know where we are going.' To S, Y said 'X was obviously pleased. I did point out in the summary that X seemed to have worked less, that his job hadn't suffered and that he had been at home more this week.' He said, 'He seems to be looking at his problems, and to understand more of what he is doing'. S said, 'This is interesting. Do you remember that after X's second session you told me, "I think X is coping with his work, but I think he'll need help in looking at what he is doing". ' Y said, 'That's a point – I'd forgotten about it.'

Comments

At a stage in his supervision, Y realised that he was not helping X as much as he might because they were not getting to the root of his problems. He understood that they all related to the use of time. S suggested that Y, with X's agreement, might take the initiative and structure the session differently so that the central subject was the use of time, and all discussion could be centred on it. This was a new approach for Y. It turned out to be what X wanted and needed, and Y found that a wide range of X's problems were then discussed, but throughout all of these X was thinking about his use of time. In the last session discussed, Y had developed his structuring of sessions. By this time X, who still had difficulties about time, was beginning to describe actions which he had taken to help himself – a plan of work, time off to attend a course, helping the club to continue without him, helping a group to work out its own problem, finding another helper. Y realised that this was happening, and wanted X to realise it too. So he introduced a summary at the end of a session, which showed how much they had achieved in the session, and how much X had achieved in his work. This structuring of the session gave Y more opportunity to help X, and it is probable that it also helped X, through experiencing this structure, to understand a value of organisation.

But there were still occasions when Y moved ahead of X, and pointed out a mistake instead of helping X to see for himself what he had done, and one occurred in the session described. S attempted to help Y to see for himself what he had done. Y quickly understood this, and with the help of analogies began to work out how he, as a supervisor, learned, describing both difficulties and insights. S tried to use what Y was saying by pin-pointing the difference between spontaneity in sessions and thinking and analysis outside sessions. At the end of the session, S did the same for Y as Y had done for X – reminded him of what he had achieved. In these sessions, therefore, Y was acquiring techniques and using them according to X's requirements. At the same time he was learning more about himself and himself as a supervisor. In developing all these aspects, Y was acquiring skill in supervising.

SOME CONCLUSIONS

In order to demonstrate in this report how workers learned to supervise, it was necessary to separate the different factors in supervising – first, the needs, feelings and attitudes of the worker/supervisor; second, the feelings and attitudes of the supervisees; third, difficulties to be overcome in supervising; fourth, workers learning to care about and understand the needs of the supervisees; fifth, workers understanding their own behaviour as supervisors; sixth, workers acquiring and understanding the techniques they used to help the supervisees to learn, and the knowledge on which they were able to draw.

But most of these factors were being learned by a worker at the same time and were being considered in each session of his own supervision. Inevitably this meant that in the early stages a worker was groping to understand what supervision was about. Insights were being accumulated, but they didn't relate to each other, and for a while workers continued in faith that they would be able to understand what they were doing, and be in control of it through understanding. It was not an easy period to go through, and the supervisor could not prevent it; she could only support the workers as they went through it, and help them understand at points where they were able to do so.

After a few months, one worker after another began to understand different factors more clearly. Usually this stage was heralded with the comment, 'I am enjoying supervising'. Then followed a long period when workers were able to understand and begin to relate factors, but were not necessarily able to use this knowledge in all aspects of their supervising. They understood what they wanted to do and how it might be done, but were not always able to do it. This produced a second period of frustration for some, and a period of interest and concentration for others. At the time of writing this report, three workers have not yet practised supervising trained leaders although one of these will do so in the immediate future. Four others are still in this second stage of supervising, in which they are able to help a supervise in many ways, understand his needs, their own difficulties, and the ways in which they are being helpful. But they need practice in using their knowledge in sessions, and in relating it, so that they are able to be spontaneous in their use of the knowledge. Three workers have now gone beyond this stage, and their learning has become the development of skill, based on an understanding of the different factors and how they relate, and on an ability to use this knowledge.

Three workers were able to work with two supervisees, and this appeared to be valuable. Not only were they able to understand more clearly where some of the difficulties encountered were those of the supervisee rather than their own, but they were also able to take the initiative more quickly with the second supervise and this appeared to speed Lip the rate of progress in learning.

When the leaders/supervisees met together to evaluate supervision they made three sets of comments relating to their problems on starting work, their feelings about being supervised and their understanding of supervision. In one, supervisees commented on their confusion – that they had not known where they were going, that they hadn't known what they knew or didn't know, that they hadn't been able to relate college and work, that their relationships with adults and superiors had been precarious, that they had been worried that they might go back to what they had been before. Another set of comments showed supervisees expressing their relief at being able to talk about their troubles, their annoyance at not being told when they were right or wrong, and at the worker/supervisor's unwillingness to become involved in their clubs by visiting and making suggestions. Some thought it must be impossible for a supervisor to understand them and their work if he didn't visit clubs. Other supervisees thought it had been more helpful to have no comeback and no visits, even though they hadn't liked it at first. Those who had been supervised for longer periods brought out the helpfulness of the method of training which they had resisted at first, and which some newer supervisees were still feeling strongly about.

This then led to a consideration of supervision, and the more experienced pointed out how supervision changed from being a session where troubles were poured out to one in which they were helped to evaluate, to see their work more clearly, and not necessarily concentrate on problems. They commented on the need for help in supervision on practical problems which they couldn't deal with, and also stressed how supervision had helped them to see a great deal in their work, of which they had been unaware. Because of the different stages of the supervisees, they were then able to consider some of the changes in themselves and in their use of supervision over a period of a year. This evaluation indicated trends and developments in supervision similar to those in the supervision of the original workers, though it also indicated the greater emotional involvement and the more urgent needs of the new leaders, as compared with the more experienced workers who had come to terms with some of their environment before being supervised.

The supervision of new leaders had therefore followed a pattern similar to that of the original workers, and the approach had been similar too. But an evaluation on an individual basis would have shown also the differences in approach and techniques, for no two supervisors were the same. This is an important, and perhaps final, factor in considering the development of skill in supervising. The project supervisor had wondered at the beginning if she would be able to help workers to develop their own skill in supervising, and to do so in their own way, knowing they must have been influenced by her supervising. It seemed that by using the methods described in this chapter, this could be done. Although, for reasons stated earlier, supervision was basically the same, the workers were individual supervisors and began to contribute to theories of supervising from their own learning and practice. The project supervisor understood more about supervision as she noted how workers handled supervision in different ways, which sometimes appeared more useful to the supervisee than her own approach might have been. At the same time, workers started to discuss with each other their opinions on the usefulness of different approaches, for example, the use of structuring and evaluation.

It was at this stage that the value of practice as a means of training supervisors became evident, for although it was acccepted that there was much more to learn, most workers were able from practice to recognise how they wanted to continue to learn, and to begin to theorise from practice − an indication that workers would not only develop skill in supervising, but would contribute to an ongoing debate about supervision in youth work.

CHAPTER ELEVEN

Evaluation

IN order to evaluate the work of the project, at least three aspects had to be considered – the workers' learning, development and increased effectiveness, the development of skill in supervising, and supervision as a form of training. The means used to evaluate were ongoing evaluation and evaluation sessions.

There are at least two ways of evaluating learning. The first is to decide on standards to be reached, and then consider a person's performance in relation to that standard. Examinations appear to be a recognised means of finding out if a person has achieved a required standard, but there are other less easily recognisable means of evaluating in this way. In each instance the standards come first and the person second.

A second way of evaluating is to start with the person, not his performance but his ability, his possible potential, his strengths and his weaknesses. A decision must then be made as to which direction he is moving in, what he wants, expects and needs to learn, and the ways in which such learning can be developed. These then provide the criteria from which to evaluate his learning. The evaluation is made by comparing the person's participation at one point with his participation at the next point and reflecting these on to the criteria in order to decide whether he has made progress. In this method the criteria are used as a sounding board, and the main concern is with the person. This was the method used in the project. To anticipate the discussion of this chapter, in summary, evaluation is defined as a process in which changes are noted and assessed in terms of the balance of strengths and weaknesses in a person or a situation.

CRITERIA FOR EVALUATION

The criteria used or evaluation came from the needs of the worker as expressed or understood, from the assumptions on which the project was based, and from new assumptions based on new understanding as the project developed. One assumption was that supervision would help a worker to accept himself, and make decisions and take action within an increasing area of understanding and awareness. Several criteria were established for this aspect of learning:

(a) Ability to use the relationship between himself and the supervisor in order to meet his own needs in learning
(b) Independence of the approval or disapproval of supervisor
(c) Independence of other people's opinions
(d) Recognition and acceptance of personal feelings
(e) Recognition and acceptance of personal values
(f) Recognition and acceptance of personal strengths and weaknesses in knowledge and skill
(g) Ability to understand what must be accepted in his behaviour, how he wants to change, and how he can change

These criteria related to the worker himself, but they were then repeated in a different form in relation to his understanding of and attitudes to the people with whom he was working:

(a) Ability to use the relationship between himself and others in order that they could meet their needs (and help relationships between others)
(b) Ability to accept other people, to recognise their right to independence, to opinions, to values, to feelings
(c) Acceptance of the contribution of other people, in terms of knowledge and skill
(d) Ability to understand what must be accepted from other people, how they want to change, and how they might be helped to change

Chapter 5 pointed up the need for a worker to understand his own role, and the situation in which he was working. This elicits, therefore, more criteria from which to evaluate learning, development and effectiveness:

The Situation
Ability to understand:
(a) The purpose of the work, and differing expectations of it
(b) The authority in a club setting, the functions of different groups and their relation to each other
(c) the different values in the club setting, and their impact on each other
(d) the club in terms of the community in which it exists
(e) individual, group and inter-group behaviour
(f) the needs of members, the contributions they are prepared to make, the facilities and help they require
(g) what must be accepted in the situation, what can be changed, and how it can be changed

Role and Function

Ability to understand:

(a) the variety of expectations of himself as a worker, and to know where he can meet these expectations and where he can not

(b) himself in relation to all individuals and groups within and connected with his centre

(c) when to help individuals in their relationships, when to help a group achieve a task, when he is training a group and when he is administrating

(d) when to take the initiative, when to leave it to others, how to co-operate, and how to resolve conflict

(e) when a decision is his, when it is that of a group, when he should carry out a decision and when he should help to change it

(f) for himself, the meaning of professional behaviour

After consideration of the areas in which a worker wanted to learn, there was yet another area for evaluation, related to Chapters 6, 7, 8, 9 and 10 on learning and skills – how did workers learn, and what skills did they develop.
The criteria were:

Ability to:

(a) distinguish between fact and opinion

(b) recognise praise or blame arising from feelings and follow this up with thinking about a situation

(c) observe, and widen range of information from which to observe

(d) think about observations and apply theories

(e) add to theories from considered conclusions of situations

(f) develop insights into behaviour and use them and act upon them

(g) analyse a situation, say what he did and felt, and keep these two separate

(h) stay on a topic and work through it

(i) understand professional skills, be confident in using them, and develop new ones

(j) relate insights, situations, or pieces of knowledge to each other

(k) use recording as a tool for learning and considered action.

Other criteria, relating particularly to learning to supervise, were:

Ability to:

(a) relax

(b) listen and pay attention

(c) care about supervisee and understand his needs, and handle own pressures and feelings in order to do so

(d) understand and use techniques, and understand the knowledge from which to draw.

The evaluation began with the supervisor's reflection on each session and on records of it. In the early sessions she was learning (as described in Chapters 4 and 8), about the worker. What did he understand? What did he want to understand? What did he need to understand? The answers to these questions came in simple terms at first. Along with examples of ability and confidence, there came to light a need for approval, a confusion between fact and opinion, a difficulty in working with a management committee. But the reflection was not only on the worker but also on the supervisor's action – where had she been helpful? Where had she not been helpful? The answers to these questions were determined by the worker's reactions to the supervisor's comments, and sometimes the answers were not known.

Reflection on each session, therefore, and reflection over several sessions brought out two forms of evaluation – the points at which the supervisor was able to help and the ways in which she could do so, and the points at which a worker was able to learn and the ways in which he could do so. For example, it became evident that A could not at one stage take the initiative but needed help in developing confidence. Because of this the supervisor could not remain silent, but needed to make suggestions. Evaluation was therefore of the ability of the worker to learn, and of the supervisor to help, and of one in relation to the other.

From points of learning and help, evaluation moved on to a consideration of progress. This meant noting that which happened and that which was said compared with that which had transpired earlier.

EXAMPLE 1

PROGRESS IN LEARNING

H said he did not know how to describe his club to the management committee in terms that they would understand and find acceptable. At this time H's comments also indicated that he was vague in his understanding of group behaviour. A few weeks later the supervisor recorded, 'H' discussed the report he had prepared for the management committee. In it, he described the needs and activities of the members clearly, showing that he now understands the connection between activities and relationships in groups. Between these two occasions there had been a seminar on relationships and activities in groups. In relating all these factors, three changes in H were noted: (a) H understood more about groups, (b) H had been able to relate theory to his experience with members, and find meaning in it, (c) H was able to describe the need of the members to the management committee in a concise form. These changes were reflected on to the criteria, and it could be seen that H had made progress in learning about groups, in relating theory to practice, and in analysing.

The understanding of a worker's progress in learning was normally reflected onto his work with the question, 'How has this insight affected the job he is doing?' Frequently this had to be answered by noting the ways in which a worker was doing his job or describing it, and comparing this with earlier methods and descriptions. But the approach to this evaluation was the same – it was in terms of changes in the worker.

EXAMPLE 2

INCREASED EFFECTIVENESS BASED ON INCREASED UNDERSTANDING

K, who was doing detached work, discussed his voluntary helpers on several occasions. He saw them as responsible people who could get to know young people, provide useful information, and extend the range of the work. They had attended training sessions with an outside person. These had not been satisfactory and K said it made too much demand on the volunteers and was unnecessary. He described problems which he had with volunteers and the lack of communication became evident. K began to see that problems need not have reached crisis points if they had been discussed earlier, but he still gave several reasons for not training the volunteers. He realised these were not his real reasons and eventually he said he didn't feel able to train a group. The subject was dropped and groups of members were discussed. A few weeks later K sent in a record of a training session which he had led, and the following weeks were devoted to discussion of his training of volunteers.

Comments

K was adamant about not training his volunteers. A few weeks later he was training them. In between he had discussed his problems, and the volunteers' needs, and had begun to understand his own attitude and feelings about training. The point of decision and the reasons for it were not known to the supervisor at that stage. Her evaluation of increased effectiveness was that whereas K has resisted meeting the needs of his volunteers, of which he had been partially aware, now he was able to meet them. The evaluation was not made from a criterion that all volunteers need training, but from K's understanding and ability to deal with a new aspect of his situation.

EXAMPLE 3

INCREASED EFFECTIVENESS BASED ON INCREASED UNDERSTANDING

E was a worker with ideas. He talked of developing a community club, and introduced new activities and schemes, usually because they seemed good ideas which he wanted to put across, rather than because there was evidence of need or interest. This was mentioned in supervision on only one occasion. In his sessions over several months, E described individuals and groups, indicating his increasing involvement with members, and increasing understanding of behaviour. Activities started which E would not previously have considered, and their value was understood by E. Constant trouble with neighbours brought contact with them, and E suggested that two might be invited to the management committee. A nearby educational establishment required premises, and E offered his by day. This led to co-operative effort in work with young people.

Comments

In supervision E was learning to observe what was happening, to understand behaviour and needs. He was also understanding more about his own behaviour, and new possibilities in his relationships. He began to react to needs and to people's ability to contribute, and his ideas became the outcome of these instead of being a result of his need to express himself. The evaluation of effectiveness was seen, not in terms of the activities and developments which could be observed, but in terms of E's increased ability to understand his situation, recognise the needs and potential within it, and take action in relation to these. Again, the change in E and in his work was reflected onto the sounding board of the criteria stated, and as a result he was seen to have become more effective in his work.

As these examples accumulated, it became possible to understand the ways and areas in which workers learned most easily, and the ways and areas which they found more difficult. Evaluation of this kind, therefore, produced a constant assessment of need, as well as a constant assessment of progress. it was important, however, to keep such evaluation to the specific instances. To generalise from the specific was unhelpful and usually misguided. It was only after long periods during which the specific examples accumulated and were understood that some conclusions could be drawn about progress.

THE WORKER'S EVALUATION

The workers too were evaluating constantly in terms of the helpfulness of supervision, their own progress, and their potential for supervising and ability to supervise. At first they asked themselves such questions as, 'I am not getting any advice or direction – is this good or bad?' 'Do I like it or don't I?' or, 'I can't make notes on what happened in supervision. Is there something wrong with me or with supervision?' At this period, the value of supervision was estimated in terms of the workers' feelings, their likes and dislikes, and their progress as they understood progress. To some, progress meant new facts or theories, to some, a sorting out of problems. The supervisor tried to help workers to understand the criteria from which they were already evaluating, and then to look for evidence of progress, and for criteria with which to assess the evidence.

There were two extremes in the approach to evaluation, with several workers at different points between them. At one end were those who wanted to spend a lot of time discussing what was happening, what they were learning, and the stage that was being reached. They believed there was a standard to be acquired, and were more concerned with reaching it than with understanding their situation. At the other end were those who wanted to get on with discussion of their work, and avoided any kind of evaluation in sessions. It was important, therefore, that evaluation should be used individually. Some workers had to work out why they wanted constant evaluation, others to be encouraged to consider what was happening from time to time.

Perhaps it is important to clarify the difference between a worker's ongoing learning in supervision and his evaluation of his learning within it. For example, in one session C described her difficulties with some of the helpers in her centre. The helpers, their contributions, their relation with C were discussed, and also C's feelings about them and the points at which conflicts arose. At the end of the session C could see, among other factors, that one helper was running an activity club within the centre, and that she saw him as a rival, that others were prepared to come into the centre, teach a particular activity and leave, and that others who were not sure what they should do, were willing to accept help and advice from C. C realised that clashes arose sometimes because she expected more interest from some, who were unaware of her expectation, and sometimes because when a helper had confidence and influence, she resented it and saw it as a challenge to her authority. C then considered action she might take to improve communication. Through all of this C was presenting, discussing and learning about her centre and herself within it, but at no time was she thinking about herself learning in supervision (here am I learning in this session – what progress am I making?).

But some weeks later, C was talking about the improved situation with the helpers, and explained what she had had to understand about herself and about the helpers before this could come about. It was then possible for C to follow her learning and development from her recognition of the problem, and to evaluate it in terms of her insights into her own behaviour and that of the helpers, and her ability as a result to take action to resolve the conflict. In the first instance C was involved in learning, in the second she was evaluating her learning. It was important that workers should be able to do both, so that they could develop insights and also understand how to evaluate when supervising.

Most frequently workers' evaluation was in one sentence. 'Over the last weeks I have realised that one has to live within the club as it is. To think "if only this, or if only that" doesn't help me to change things.' 'I used to say the members wanted to be treated like adults. It suddenly hit me that for the first time I am treating them that way – that's why there are so many of them, and they are so active.' Sometimes such comments were left without discussion. Sometimes they were examined. As the project developed, most workers became less concerned with evaluating their learning and more involved in their learning. When this happened, the supervisor felt more able to introduce incidental evaluation, not in order to help them assess themselves, but as a preparation for the time when they would be supervising. She would ask questions leading to evaluation: 'Do you realise how differently you are now describing members? – or recording? or working with the management committee? What has happened?' This method was also occasionally used to help a worker think about supervision. 'What happened to the advice I gave you last week?' 'I didn't take it', or 'Have you considered the point of my asking those questions?' Sometimes, as the supervision practice drew nearer, a whole session was analysed in order to evaluate the points where it was helpful and the points where it was not.

Mutual evaluation then required a balance, first so that workers could become involved in their learning, and at the same time have some sense of progress; second, so that workers could experience being supervised and also learn to analyse and evaluate it.

EVALUATION SESSIONS

On two occasions, sessions were allocated to an evaluation. The first time, each worker had an evaluation session. The second time, some workers used a few minutes of a session for evaluation, others a whole session.

On the first occasion, that is, after the first ten sessions, it must be admitted that the supervisor was wondering how far her own evaluations were realistic, and decided that comments from the workers would be helpful to her. She also believed that some workers would welcome the opportunity to have a full discussion on what was happening, but this was not a primary reason for it. Workers were asked beforehand to work out what they now understood by supervision, aspects which they found helpful or unhelpful, and any differences which it had made to their learning or work. Most workers simply sat down and talked in their sessions, with very little comment from the supervisor, working out what they meant as they went along. The following are extracts from two evaluations.

EVALUATION BY H

'Helpful – because no clothes pegs. Previously worked on instinct, but am now changing; have learned to design records to help me see what is happening. Previously looked at one large group – now see sub-groups and individuals. Take more notice of the part individuals play in making groups behave the way they do. Previously hit and miss relationships. Would never have thought about fringe members – last week explained to some that I hadn't much time, to spend with them, but I knew they were all right and if they wanted anything would they tell me.

I'm beginning to explain what is going on.

I haven't done justice to the management committee before.

I'm becoming more aware of the worker in co-operation with other workers.

I don't now explain things in black and white – am finding more acceptable ways of describing things.

I guess I'm now accepting the circumstances in which I find myself.

It has been a reassessment of myself in relation to my job and role, with other people contributing (supervisor and group). There are question marks and these make one ask oneself other questions.

Supervision. At the outset it was a vote of confidence – my acceptance to the project was important.

The questioning of someone from outside the club setting was important.

I had confidence in talking frankly.

Practical side – recording. I didn't know how to make them concise and useful.

Learned about myself in relation to people outside.

Techniques – You want to gain my confidence so you let me do most of the talking.

I think maybe you encouraged me to record, wanting to know about the person recording them.

I was a bit concerned about recording, anxious to know how to do it.

I think you were helping me to get to the real pressures and to find out where they were.

I felt supported, and you encouraged me to do things.

You didn't criticise or disapprove – and that would have led to compromise and glossing over.'

EVALUATION BY F

'The most important thing is that I can think about a situation now – that

I can even think. I see things more objectively – I am not wondering how they would affect me.

I have sorted out my own role, so it doesn't worry me so much as to how things affect me.

When I first came I wondered if my material for supervision was the same as the others – I doubted if I would fit in. Then I realised it was no good worrying, the point was that I could come in at my own level. I didn't at first know what supervision was about, and I used to try to think what problems I should bring. I was in a muddle and a state most of the time – I thought I ought to be in a muddle, and if a worker wasn't, something must be wrong. I realise now it meant I could blame everyone else then. I expected someone to give answers, to say do this or that, and to reassure – I didn't get any of it.

I got support in an odd sort of way – I think that's how I came to be able to work things out for myself.

I no longer worry so much about what people think of me. Now I find I have been able to admit to people when I think I've been stupid.

Previously I felt out on a limb, and I realise how helpful it's been to have someone to recognise my problems, and help, with no prejudices and no strings attached.

I used to think one recorded only in order to work out problems. I realise this meant I didn't even notice the non-problems. I think this is partly why some of the members who presented no problems have left the club.

I used to expect you to 'chip in' and when you didn't, I got irritated a bit, but decided you must know what you are doing.'

These evaluations were a series of thoughts and feelings, which included a number of unspoken questions about what the supervisor was doing, and what was happening to themselves. At this stage few workers were able to express outright their mixed feelings about it, although some of these were drawn out later in discussion. On balance, the evaluations indicated that the workers were prepared to accept the kind of help offered in supervision, because it had opened up new areas of understanding. They were not particularly concerned with the technicalities which some were beginning to understand in varying degrees, but were more interested in the experience.

At this stage in the project the supervisor contributed in two ways to the workers' evaluation. She discussed and explored points which workers indicated they were not sure about, and would like to understand. In a few instances she discussed, and sometimes drew out, areas in which a worker would like or need to concentrate. But she believed that it would be unhelpful to allocate more sessions for evaluation until there was a specific purpose.

The second evaluation occurred, therefore, when the workers were about to supervise, and was a consideration of how far they were prepared to do so.

After some months of supervision, the supervisor's thoughts had turned to the possibility of workers being able to supervise. She began to ask such questions as, 'Can he relax in his work with individuals? Can he listen? Could he support a supervisee without telling him what to do? Will he be able to present and record supervision sessions realistically so that he can learn as he supervises? Does he understand his own work and himself in relation to it? Is he able to handle problems and pressures in his work? How far is he able to handle his own feelings?' In an attempt to answer these questions, evidence of learning and development from previous evaluation had to be brought to bear on them, and all aspects were considered in terms of each worker. There was no question of a worker reaching an overall standard, but each question had to be asked about him. No worker understood all his work and himself in relation to it, to the extent that he could not learn more. To one, the incentive of supervising might help him to record realistically; to another, relaxation in supervision might come only from experience. So the supervisor's evaluation in terms of preparedness for supervising was an assessment of the individual, his ability, and the progress he appeared to have made in relation to the criteria.

The workers had also been thinking about supervising. Some were asking questions similar to those of the supervisor. Others were feeling more emotional about it, either wanting to supervise because they thought they ought to be ready, or not wanting to start because they were fearful of doing so. All had mixed feelings about supervising. The evaluation sessions, which were individual, were therefore discussions about evidence of preparedness and about feelings. They did not all occur at the same time, but were arranged at the suggestion of either the supervisor or worker. According to the discussion about supervising which a worker might have had previously, the sessions lasted for periods varying from half an hour to two hours.

Two workers, in their evaluation, realised that although they wanted to supervise, evidence suggested they were not ready to do so – they found listening difficult, and knew they would not be able to resist giving answers and suggesting what workers should do. As they were already responsible for their own staff, they decided to try to help them individually instead of attempting to supervise new workers.

A was one of the workers who, in order to give himself confidence, wrote down his understanding of the role he should take as a supervisor. He then discussed his paper, describing what he meant by each item and considering his own ability to carry out his own suggestions. The following is A's original paper:

'What I see my role in supervision to be, and the techniques I will use.
Building up of confidence.
Support to the leader in the work he is doing at all times (non-judgemental), hearing and understanding his needs.
Recognising that he knows his job and is coming to supervision on equal terms and that his contribution is valid and essential.
Facilitating the bringing of his experiences to the supervision.
To help him understand what supervision is and its relevance when it is work related.
Find out what the leader wants to do in any situation rather than give what I would do, i.e. when confronted with "What would you do to get out of this?"find out what lie wants to do and work out with him what effect this would have and so to look more closely at the problem.
To take the initiative to stimulate action when necessary. To act, maybe, as a stimulus for making records. To help him to observe, to crystallise these observations and to use them for a basis for discussion.
To help him see how social group work relates to the work he is doing (not v.v.).
In most of the above I am in the role of observer (not watching) but using the material he brings to the session to help him develop his professional understanding, also to help him to get into the habit of professional thinking about his work.
While I am doing the supervising, understanding my own influence on him and the possible effects this will have. Appreciating that the conclusion of discussion by his coming to a decision on some issue is the right one, even though it may not be the one that I would make.
All through the supervision, observing the ethics and principles of our profession.'

EVALUATION IN RELATION TO THE PURPOSE OF THE PROJECT

The evaluation to this point has all been in relation to the purpose of supervision – to help a worker to increase his understanding and his effectiveness in his work. The worker's learning, and the helpfulness of supervision to him, were evaluated together, and in specific terms. But the project had two main purposes – to help workers acquire techniques in supervising, and to prepare a report on the project, and material decribing the nature of supervision. It is these which now require consideration.

The project revealed the minor importance of techniques compared with the number of factors to be understood in order to supervise effectively. Therefore the workers were helped to acquire skill in supervising, of which techniques were only a part. It would be easy to say that workers are developing skill in supervising, seven now, and one more to begin soon. But this development had to be assessed in the same way as the evaluation of learning – in terms of individual progress.

The project supervisor's evaluation of progress in developing skill was in relation to the worker's discovery of the factors to be understood – acceptance and support of a supervisee, learning from a supervisee, overcoming difficulties, practising and acquiring techniques, and the knowledge on which to draw. Understanding and using these factors was seen as developing skill, and each worker progressed according to his own ability and perception.

When the workers first started to supervise, they wanted to evaluate themselves as supervisors. Again, this was usually for emotional reasons – were they good enough, how did they compare with others? Such concern usually inhibited their supervising, and they were encouraged to become involved in supervising, and to consider themselves only in relation to that situation. When they were able to do this, they began to recognise the factors to be understood, and to find material and criteria with which to evaluate supervision.

At this stage, workers became less concerned with themselves personally – they knew what they were able to do – and were more concerned with understanding new aspects of supervision. Gradually, as they understood the factors in relation to each other, so they began to evaluate their supervising in terms of its helpfulness to the supervisee – in specific terms. This was evaluation as described at the beginning of this chapter – the wheel had come full circle.

There was no way of determining a dividing line at which one changed from the non-supervisor to the supervisor, or from the supervisor to the skilled supervisor. An evaluation of today could be changed by the insight of tomorrow. Experience showed that insights could quickly change ability and skill in several directions at once. It also showed that a long period of development, learning and acquiring skill, could be followed by a period on a plateau. Workers would say that although they are given the title in certain circumstances, and although they have spent two years learning to supervise, their qualification for supervising continues to be determined by their effectiveness in helping individual leaders, and their understanding of what they are doing. To this end they continue to practise and examine their practice.

The second purpose of the project was to prepare a report on the project, and material on the nature of supervision in youth work. This report, which is based on the full participation of everyone concerned, presents the two aspects in one. The first is a description of what happened in the project, taken from different angles. The second is an analysis of what was happening – that which was learned in the project. The two are interwoven throughout, but it is hoped that it is possible to detect the difficulties, the problems and the progress, and the factors affecting them – and thus to see, in these terms, supervision as a method of training being used to meet the needs of youth workers, and helping them develop skill in supervising.

CHAPTER TWELVE

Some Conclusions

THIS project was only one of a great variety of developments within the youth service, and it seems that conclusions could be most usefully drawn out about the particular function of supervision compared with other training, and also ways in which it could be used to meet differing needs. This is being done by attempting to answer some of the questions that have been asked of the project.

'What is the value of supervision compared with other forms of training?'

There are two aspects of training with which supervision might be compared – the first is other training in the field, and the second is basic training. In the first aspect, most of the training available consists of occasional weekend or seven-day courses, or extra-mural courses. Also, in some areas, attempts are being made to change staff gatherings from administrative meetings to training sessions. All of these have their particular value in helping workers to share and exchange knowledge and develop new knowledge and skill, and to gain more understanding of themselves in relation to each other. The particular value of supervision is that it is based on a face-to-face relationship; for once the worker is not a member of a group for training.

There are few opportunities for any person carrying a responsible job with people, to have someone who will listen to and be interested in his problems, his difficulties and his needs, and to know that the 'someone' is available regularly to help him through his own particular ups and downs. The need for individual help is recognised in many different settings, and apart from social casework, is being met by an upsurge of 'counselling' in schools, marriage, and crises of different kinds. Although much of the counselling is to help people with difficult personal problems, in some settings it is being used to help individuals in the early stages of difficulty, before a crisis is reached, and to prevent it.

The youth worker is expected to be a stable person, usually able to handle his own personal problems. But he is in a responsible job, under pressure, and constantly helping with other people's problems, as well as providing an environment in which young people can be helped in their growing up and to enjoy doing so. He too needs to be significant somewhere, not in terms of an image of what he should be, but as the person, the worker, that he is. The first difference in the training provided by supervision, therefore, is that in being a face-to-face relationship it recognises the significance of John Smith, person and youth worker. For once he does not have to adapt himself to the needs of a group. He can relax and get help.

The relationship is, however, ongoing, as meetings continue regularly whether or not the worker has a problem. Here is one of the differences between counselling which is normally problem-centred, and supervision which is work-centred and a form of training. If a worker were to meet a supervisor only when he had problems he would have a very different idea of himself, and himself in relation to the supervisor. He might well see himself as a person of problems, and the supervisor as the person to help him when in difficulties. But through regular meetings, he is also able to examine and learn from achievements unrelated to any problem, and knows that within this relationship his competence is understood as well as his difficulties. His offering of himself within the relationship is therefore more balanced – he comes as a person who knows, as well as a person in need, a person with strengths as well as weaknesses. Supervision then as an ongoing individual relationship accepts that the whole person, the stable person, the professional worker, has a need to be significant. Through the understanding of this, the relationship can be used for fruitful learning, leading to more relaxed work and a greater acceptance and understanding of the needs of others.

It is sometimes suggested that group training would be equally useful and would require fewer people. Group training as complementary to supervision is described in Appendix One, but perhaps one aspect could be pointed up here. The concentration on individual needs and learning, even though frequently other people and situations are being discussed, is in itself an experience for the worker, for which no amount of discussion about 'the importance of the individual' can be a substitute. His own acceptance appears to have a snowballing effect, which can be far-reaching in the help and training he offers to other people.

While groups are valuable in a variety of ways, much of a group's time can be spent in the early days in a struggle for individual needs to be met. For new workers in a complex setting, the outcome might never be satisfactory. At the same time, individual training is not seen as a substitute for group training or group meetings, but as an addition to it. It is groups of workers who will continue to support and help each other, long after regular individual help has come to an end. These points are made, however, to suggest that methods of training might be studied in terms of their relative value, rather than on the basis of economy.

In the other aspect – supervision and basic training – the first is seen as complementary to the second. While an emphasis in basic training is on understanding other people's ideas, theories and conclusions, with limited opportunities for learning from practice, the emphasis in supervision is on learning from practice, and then relating the learning to other theories. Although there is obviously a place for learning in both ways, the relative importance of each is not yet clear within the youth service. But supervision is perhaps one way of providing a discipline for learning from practice, sometimes helping a worker to learn from 'interesting' experience instead of by 'bitter' experience.

When learning from the situation, the worker's contribution to his own learning is positive or active from the beginning. He has to observe and think about his observations, otherwise there is no material for him to discuss and learn from. As he continues to do this, with help, so his own range of information from which to observe and think is continually increasing by his own efforts. His learning does not begin and end in a session, but is happening between sessions. It is also closely related to and/or about his own actions. The worker cannot criticise, laugh at, or applaud someone else from his point of observation, for he is confronted by himself in his observations. He can, therefore, learn to understand, with help, how he behaves, and the results of his actions. This means that the worker cannot depend on intellectual learning, because being involved, he recognises his feelings and values, and finds that he wants to learn how to deal with these and use them.

Learning from a situation, therefore, has value in at least two particular ways. It means that any new insights or understanding are the worker's own. He learns to perceive meaning in a situation for himself, and is therefore on the way to being able to explain it to other people with understanding and conviction. Secondly, because of his involvement as he learns, he is enabled to use all of himself in his learning, and to understand how to use all of himself, with awareness, in his work. Although supervision is by no means alone in providing the setting for learning of this kind, it is perhaps the place where it can be done with the greatest concentration.

'Did you produce a general pattern for recording?'

In one sense the answer to this question is yes, in that most workers found value in writing down what happened, in questioning the description, in analysing it, and in drawing conclusions about it. But otherwise no general pattern emerged, and one reason for this is related to two of the purposes in recording which tend to cancel each other out.

If a worker wants to record in order to keep his finger on the pulse of the club, to remind himself of certain facts, to consider appropriate action, or to draw certain conclusions from a series of records, then such is the complexity of his job that he wants to find a way of gathering and writing down as much information as possible, about as many people and situations as possible, in the least possible time. He then wants a pattern, a check sheet – some means of achieving this task.

If a worker wants to learn about himself in his situation he wants to use records as an added tool with which to learn. This means that as the range of information from which he learns increases, so his records expand; as he understands the difference between facts and opinions, so the content of his records changes; as he wants to look at himself as well as his members, so he includes himself in his records. Frequently he learns to analyse his work through his analysis of records. He can rarely hope to cover the whole club through recording in this way, though he can learn to relate insights to different situations.

If a worker has both purposes in mind when recording, he can be pulled in two different directions – to condense and to expand – and he is likely to achieve neither. If, however, he sets out with the second purpose in mind, it is possible that after a long period of work, he will understand what he wants to record and the reasons for it, and will find his own means of achieving the first purpose. In the project, workers wanted to learn, and to use records to train themselves (though not everyone saw this at first), and this meant a great deal of time spent on recording. Some eventually found short cuts for particular purposes. If the emphasis had not changed to supervising, it is possible that through discussion of the records used, patterns of recording might have emerged – but these could hardly have been used as a substitute for the learning period, when recording was very much an individual process.

'How can supervision as a method of training be useful for part-time leaders?'

Supervision within the project started at a point of need. The basic assumptions pointed to areas where professional workers had needs in common, but as supervision started, so the individual needs of workers emerged. For example, all workers needed to learn more about the subject matter as described in Chapter 5. But A needed to learn particularly how to take initiative, E to become involved in relationships with members, and H to analyse his observations. Again, all workers wanted to learn, to understand more clearly the work they were doing, but the approaches to learning were individual with certain common elements. The analysis of supervision brought out constantly the need to recognise that which was common to all and that which was individual.

It might be useful, therefore, to consider the elements common to the supervision of professional and part-time workers, and the points at which there are differences. The setting – youth work – is the same. Learning in supervision is from the situation, and therefore it might be assumed that there should be little difference between the subject matter arising from the full-time worker's situation and that in which the part-time worker finds himself. If a part-time worker is responsible for work with young people on three evenings a week, and a full-time worker for similar work on five evenings, it would be difficult to assume that the former needs less understanding and knowledge than the latter. Presumably the areas of need common to the full-time workers apply equally to the part-time workers in this position, and therefore supervision could meet these needs for both categories.

But this leads to a consideration of the worker's role, for although learning in supervision is from the situation, it is also about the worker's role in that situation. This might well be where the differences based on the area of the part-time worker's responsibility become apparent. The part-time worker responsible for the work might want to understand (as the full-time worker) how to function more adequately with the management committee, whereas an assistant might want to clarify his role in relation to that of the worker responsible for the centre. An instructor might want to understand how to use his activity-skill more effectively, and a general assistant might be more interested in the needs of young people in relation to discipline. Supervision in all these examples would provide the same function as in the project – helping a worker to understand and carry out his role in his situation. As the roles and situations varied, so they would affect the discussion and the content of supervision, but not its nature.

There is one obvious difference between the professional worker and the part-time worker, and that is in the basic training. The basic training of the full-time worker is of a longer duration, and takes place before he is supervised as a professional worker. The basic training of a part-time worker is brief, and at present is usually concurrent with the supervision. One difference therefore would appear to be that the professional worker has more theory than the part-time worker, which he can apply to practice in his supervision. It could also be that the part-time worker is less able to be analytical than the professional worker, though as yet there appears to be no evidence for such a clear distinction. The implications for supervision, however, could be that the part-time worker needs more help in conceptualising from his observations, and in relating them to other experiences, and also to the rest of his training. If a part-time worker needs to learn to theorise on his observations, and to understand other people's theories about human behaviour, then perhaps the function of supervision is to help him find ways of doing so.

Another difference noted is that professional workers are carefully selected as people with the potential for learning, and for carrying responsible jobs in youth work. Part-time workers are of an infinite variety, ranging from those carrying responsible jobs in allied fields to volunteers who have come into the youth service wanting to help, and not being sure how. This indicates that the learning ability of the part-time workers is probably of a greater variety, and there might be a great number for whom this is more limited. One might find difficulty in conceptualising, but might have insight into the behaviour of young people. Another might find difficulty in understanding the skill he is using. A third might be able to absorb theories, while finding it hard to change his authoritarian approach. If the purpose of training were to acquire set standards and to absorb a particular set of knowledge, then supervision, along with other forms of training, would not achieve this end for these people. But as supervision begins at the point of individual need and ability, it is more likely to help any worker, however limited, to develop his understanding and skill where he is able to do so. Basically, where learning ability is concerned, the differences are between individuals more than between categories, and for training purposes are frequently merely a difference in degree. The starting points might be different, the language might be different, the support might take a different form, and different techniques might be used, but basically the skill required to help learning is the same in supervision whether the supervisee is a professional worker or a young volunteer.

'Is there a difference between supervising workers — part-time and full-time — and supervising students?'

Students could be part-time workers in a training course, or potential full-time workers doing practical work as part of their college training.

Although it is suggested that basically the nature of supervision would be the same, there are at least three aspects which would need careful consideration. These are the contained setting in which the student operates, the assessment which is generally accepted as essential, and the relationship between the supervisor and others responsible for the student's practice.

The student's practice is bounded by time, so that it is important for him to understand as much as possible within that time. If, for instance, a student has not previously been in a large open youth club, to leave him alone to find his own feet could well be both time-wasting and petrifying, particularly if the student feels he must do well. To be flung in at the deep end can be a useful experience, but only if someone is there to prevent one from drowning. If a supervisor sees the student each day, he is able to help him consider what he has observed, and new aspects that could be observed. If he sees him only once a week, preparation at the beginning seems indicated. This is particularly important if a student is to be left alone with a group, and responsible for it. In supervision he can work out some of the things he might expect in the group, and some of the factors to be considered, and his own feelings about it. The student therefore needs frequent supervision in which he is supported, is helped to prepare, develop his observations, reflect, and in many instances to be selective.

Normally, the work of a student is being assessed, and the student is aware of this. Here there is a difference between supervision for the student and for the worker. Inevitably the student's work and his relationship with the supervisor is affected by the knowledge that a report will be made. But experience has shown that if the student is aware that the report is to be based on a mutual evaluation by supervisor and student, and if he knows that he will discuss the report and understand what is in it, he visibly relaxes. If this happens, the knowledge of an assessment need not be a hindrance to the student's learning, but the evaluation can be a fruitful part of it.

The student's supervisor could be the warden of the centre in which he works, or a representative of the college or training agency. Sometimes it could appear that both are supervising him. Whoever is responsible for supervising, the triangle remains, as all three are involved, and therefore it seems important that the different functions are clearly defined, so that rivalry can be minimised, and the student can understand the kinds of help and authority he can expect from different sources.

'Must a supervisor be completely detached, except for the supervisory relationship, from the professional worker being supervised?'

The project indicated the value of detachment. Workers surrounded by differing expectations of their work expressed on several occasions the relief of being able to discuss it with someone who had 'no strings attached'. Although they had to experience and know for themselves that sessions were confidential, and could not merely accept a statement of this, there is little doubt that they were able to discuss some aspects of their work and behaviour because the supervisor was removed from their situation. Chapter 4 described the effect of the relationship on the content, and of the content on the relationship. The fact that the supervisor had only one role as far as the worker was concerned, and had no outside responsibilities for the worker, meant that the relationship was of the simplest possible in the circumstances, and thus provided opportunity for more fruitful and adult learning.

There is no doubt that if the supervisor has other responsibilities to the worker, the relationship, and therefore to an extent the nature of supervision, will be changed. But it is unrealistic to expect that supervision will be developed throughout the youth service on the basis of detachment. Therefore it seems essential that in arranging for supervision, the difficulties should be brought out into the open and recognised.

The more experienced and senior staff in most areas are the youth officers, and it is therefore frequently assumed that they should be the people to supervise workers. The year's extension of this project will provide the opportunity for a group of youth officers to be supervised in their own supervision of workers, and it is envisaged that some of the opportunities and difficulties will come to light. But already some difficulties are clear. The youth officer is the person responsible for ensuring that the youth work policy for an area is carried out; sometimes it is his own policy agreed by his committee, sometimes the committee's policy accepted by him, and more frequently a combination of both. Although he might well expect the participation of workers in determining policy, accept that they have their own areas of responsibility, or sympathise with unorthodox ideas and methods, he has his own job to do. When he is confronted with a new professional worker, his questions remain: 'How far can I help this worker to learn at his own pace, thinking for himself, and how far must I see that he works according to our ideas and pattern? How much, also, will one affect the other?'

The important factor is that the youth officer should recognise his two roles in relation to the worker, and understand how he can deal with them.

There is at least one other role normally assigned to the youth officer – that of assessment. It is unfortunate that the probationary year of a worker has frequently been linked with supervision, implying that supervision is not only training but includes checking on the worker to see that he does his job properly. The youth officer in the position of supervisor and assessor has to come to terms with the possible effects of one upon the other. If his supervision of the worker is effective, he will learn a great deal more about him than from his other contacts, and it will not be easy for him to know how to use this information. This, of course, does not only apply to probationary workers, but to decisions on promotion, responsibility allowances, references and grants.

The main difficulty of the youth officer, therefore, is in sorting out his different roles, and in working out how these will affect his supervision (as an educational process) of a worker. Perhaps his main consideration will be how they are going to affect the worker's attitude to him in supervision. The temptation might well be for him to believe that as he (Y.O.) is sympathetic, understanding and helpful, the worker won't worry too much about it. But if a worker is feeling tentative and inadequate, or ambitious and determined, the barriers are likely to go up to the person with power, however understanding he is. This will affect the relationship and therefore the learning.

The situation of the training officers, statutory and voluntary, could be very similar to that of the youth officer, depending on the training officers' terms of reference and position with an organisation. If officials, statutory and voluntary, are supervising, an alleviation of their difficulties might be brought about if they are relieved of their administrative responsibilities and allegiances, so that they can be free to learn, and to help workers understand policies, instead of having to ensure that they are carried out.

One point seems important here. Although a complexity of roles for a supervisor will always affect supervision for the reasons stated, it is being considered here in the context of the youth service. Youth work has only recently been recognised as a profession and this might well be aggravating the problem. As the roles, purposes, and principles within it are not yet clear, there appear to be rivalries and suspicions as to how people will behave. Confidentiality, and its meaning and use, has not yet been clarified within the profession, and therefore no one is sure how information will be used.

In the project, the workers commented on their early inability to believe the statement that their sessions would be confidential. They had to experience this before they could accept it. After a long period they discussed the importance of knowing that supervision was confidential, but some said they would no longer mind if the supervisor discussed their learning with officials, and they clarified the difference between material based on evidence and reality, as compared with judgemental statements. Even so, they recognised the need for a common understanding of such material, and how it should be used in the context of the youth service. Development of this kind seems an indication that, as concepts of professional behaviour are clarified, shared and accepted within the youth service, so the attitudes to and understanding of supervision as an educational process will change, and many of the present difficulties might well be removed.

This suggestion relates, also, to the supervision of part-time paid and voluntary workers by the worker responsible for a unit. The need for clarification of roles, and for the worker to understand how the complexity of roles affects him and the part-time workers, is important in this setting. But it will be interesting to find out if supervision within centres will become acceptable and effective more easily, for although part-time workers might have attitudes, feelings, and reservations similar to those of the professional worker, there does not appear to be so much at stake for them, as they are not dependent on youth work for their livelihood.

'Who should supervise and how should they be trained?'

The project certainly could not provide answers to this question, but its experience provided several suggestions. The first is that although it is less tidy, it seems more advisable to select supervisors on their individual ability for training with this method, instead of trying to allocate supervision to particular categories of workers within the youth service. Already, professional workers in different allied fields are being used as supervisors, and there are no doubt a number of others who would be able and prepared, with or without training, to supervise youth workers if invited to do so. The danger is in asking a person to supervise *simply* because he is a good headmaster, lecturer, youth officer, youth worker or psychiatrist, though individuals within such categories might be well equipped to do so. Perhaps the first essential is to find agreement on the purpose of supervision and the methods to be used to achieve it, and from this to establish a few basic criteria for the selection of supervisors.

The ten workers within the project were selected as potential supervisors not only on their competence in their own work, but also on indications of skill, flexibility, and ability to feel, learn, think and analyse, as well as other individual factors. Of these, seven are developing skill in supervising, and possibly others will do so. But it is doubtful that they could have developed this skill without training.

At the beginning, twenty-one months seemed a long time to allocate to training. As the project developed, everyone realised it was too short a period, and two and a half years will be needed and used by most of the workers. And yet, this amounts only to approximately 100 sessions, 200 hours – the equivalent of about six weeks' work. This suggests two factors. The first is that given certain potential, it is probable that many individuals within (and/ or without) the youth service could be trained to supervise while continuing their normal jobs, but that the training requires concentration and hard work on their part. Recognition of this training as a part of their work, by officials and committees concerned, would be an important asset. A conclusion from the project is that while most workers and/or officials can and do help others in a variety of ways, skill in supervising cannot be acquired without practice, hard work, and thought, together with criteria already mentioned, and the help of a more experienced person. It also requires coming to terms with the job already being done, so that personal pressures, problems and developments are understood and dealt with. For these reasons it is suggested that the experience of being supervised, in itself, does not make a supervisor, and that it seems unhelpful to ask workers to supervise in their early years as youth workers.

The second factor is that of economy in time and personnel. Although two and a half years seems a long time, the equivalent of six weeks' full-time work might bring this into perspective as it might not in this form appear to be such a great deal of time to allocate to the mastery of new skills, and competence in a different role. While this time is being given to training, new workers are being trained and thus given the help they need, and other work can continue. It is suggested that training of this nature could be undetaken by training establishments, with the minimum of extra administration and personnel. It would not need to be restricted to supervision in youth work, but could serve workers in a variety of social work and educational settings.

As pointed out earlier, this report cannot provide the answer to the selection and training of supervisors. But if it were accepted that super-vision requires training and skill, and is not acquired automatically by reason of one's job, then perhaps it should be possible to find those people who are willing to be trained, and to recognise that the importance lies not so much in their being skilled before they start, as in training being available for them as they practise.

'Is it possible to relate supervision more closely to college training?'

Presumably the purpose of both basic training and supervision is to help the student/worker to learn, to want to learn and to be competent and effective in his work. If so, then perhaps the more important question is how far can those responsible for basic training and for supervision get together so that a situation is provided in which ongoing learning is possible and fruitful.

At this stage in the development of the youth service, the situation is so complex that it would be difficult to acquire common understanding and agreement. The basic training is at present in six different courses, as well as social science and teacher training. While there are elements common to all of these, the content, emphasis, methods and interpretation vary, so that it is difficult for supervisors to make many assumptions about basic training. At the same time, in the field there are so many attitudes to and interpretations of supervision, that it would be impossible for those responsible for basic training to train students with any expectations of a particular form of continuation. The project can draw no conclusions on this overall aspect of the situation, except that discussions and consultations should continue and be intensified, but it has thrown up specific points which might be considered.

Supervision is a form of individual training, and therefore the point at which it might meet the student training is the individual tutorial. If as many factors as possible relating to this were understood by tutors and supervisors, the workers might find supervision as the ongoing known situation during the period of transition from college to work.

The tutorial appears to be used in many different ways. It can be used to help the student in his understanding of theory, or in the sorting out of his personal and/or learning problems. It can be used by the tutor to assess the student's learning, to ensure that he is covering the area of learning required, or to bring in his observations and knowledge of the students from other settings. It can be voluntary in that a student asks for a tutorial if he wants one, or compulsory in that he attends a tutorial every week. It can be a setting in which the student brings up any problem he wants to discuss, or in which the tutor normally sets the pace and decides on the content. In some instances the tutorial covers the practical work as well as the theoretical work. In others 'supervision' is used for practical work, and is separated from tutorials.

When a student leaves college he might be prepared to work out some of his own needs in learning, using a supervisor to help him; he might feel he uses a supervisor when he feels like it or has a problem; he might expect the supervisor to make the decisions or use information about him in the sessions. Inevitably he relates his experience with his tutor to his expectations of supervision. In the field there are as many variations of supervision as there are of tutorials in college. It is the student/worker who has to adapt to that which is offered.

It appears that there are at least three possibilities for helping the student/ worker. The first is clarification and agreement about the aims of and methods used in tutorials. The second is clarification and agreement about supervision. But the most important is an understanding of how the two can relate for the benefit of the student/worker. For example, if the colleges decided that tutorials could be used to help the student to understand and determine his own needs in learning, then by the end of the course he could be doing this in his tutorials, and supervision would be a continuation, though the material would be different. If, on the other hand, the colleges decided that tutorials would fulfil a different function, and that students needed a more structured setting in which tutors set the pace, then the post-college supervisors might introduce the worker to responsibility for his own learning, gradually. The important factor is that another pressure should not be added to those which the worker is already experiencing in his new job, which means that tutors and supervisors need to come to some agreement.

The worker's stated understanding of what happened to him in college is the point from which a supervisor starts to help him, but it cannot be taken as fact, partly because this understanding changes with new awareness, and also because sometimes it has overtones arising from his new situation. The experienced supervisor might learn reasonably quickly to relate the different factors as he begins to understand the individual worker, but the new supervisor has more difficulty in recognising the factors. This situation will always arise, and the supervisor in helping the worker from the worker's points of understanding must always expect to learn mostly from the worker. But it would be a help if the supervisor could make some basic assumptions of all basic training, just as no doubt it would help those responsible for training courses to be able to make assumptions about the training available through supervision.

A conclusion therefore is that although the worker might well benefit if the supervisor understands the basic training, and can therefore help in relating it, there is need for clarification and agreement in the basic training to enable him to do so, and there is need for consultation between tutors and supervisors to enable him to see how it can be done most fruitfully.

'How long should a worker be supervised?'

If a student is in college, or is allocated practical work, his tutorials or supervision are related to the time in college or length of practice. This does not mean that the tutor or supervisor expects the student's learning to come to an end with either of these, but that his learning in that particular setting is bounded by time. The limit of time can create pressure on the learning, and without skilful teaching could hinder the learning.

At a stage in the youth service, when the time needed for basic training is by no means clear, it would be unfortunate if learning through supervision were also to have the artificial barrier of time as its limit, particularly before other factors about learning in supervision are recognised or understood. There are, however, a few points worth noting here which could have some bearing on time, without suggesting a particular limit. They are related to different purposes in supervision.

The new worker in the field needs support most of all – it is this need which emerges most strongly in his supervision. He wants to be able to discuss his difficulties and problems, and express his feelings about these, knowing that this will not be held against him. While this is happening, he needs help in understanding the situation in which he finds himself. As some workers require help of this kind for many months, supervision throughout the probationary year might well not go beyond the point of studying difficulties and problems. If supervision ends with the probationary year, they will then miss an important aspect of their learning.

After some months the workers' discussions are no longer based only on their feelings about their work, or on intellectual opinions about it. They begin to present situations which may or may not be problems, and which they can examine. It is obvious that learning of this kind can continue indefinitely, as the worker reaches a deeper understanding, or as he extends the range of knowledge of the situation, or as both happen alongside each other. But although the project experience could not indicate in general terms how long supervision should or should not be used to help such learning, at least two factors emerged. First, for at least two workers, many factors seemed to fall into place only after two years, and this might indicate a longer period for others. It was after this period that the workers were able to work quite differently and confidently in groups, with colleagues, as workers and as supervisors. Second, there is evidence that if the supervisor is constantly helping the worker to think for himself, make his own decisions and take his own actions, so the worker is widening the area in which he feels competent to learn and take action without help. So the areas where supervision is needed become more clearly defined, and the worker knows when he requires only infrequent consultations. Time then appears to be dependent on the worker's needs, on the supervisor's role, on the understood purpose, on the relationship, and on the worker's ability to learn – among other factors.

Supervision is seen as an opportunity to relate practice and theory. This also affects the time factor. Experience has shown that such relating rarely happens realistically in the early months, and for some it takes much longer. Frequently theories lie dormant, or are rejected, while the worker gets on with his work, relating it to his experience before college and/or pointing out the irrelevance of college teaching. Or a worker starts out by applying theories which don't work out, becomes frustrated and then rejects them for a while. It is only when he begins to understand his situation from his observations (possibly using theories of which he is unaware) and becomes relaxed in it, that he is prepared and able to bring theory and practice together. Contrary to some expectations, therefore, the value of supervision in relating theory and practice does not emerge in the early stages, if sessions are based on the worker's needs.

Just as deciding on a particular length of time for supervision would bear no relation to the needs of individual workers, so a personal decision by a worker that he no longer needed supervision could be equally unreal. He could be annoyed that he needed help, he might compare himself with other workers, he could be pressured by other demands, he might not be getting the help he required in supervision. With such reasons, a worker would have to make his own decision, but the point is that it could not be assumed in all cases that a worker would know when supervision would no longer be helpful – his judgements could be emotional at that moment.

It seems therefore that the new factors mentioned here indicate much more exploration into the contribution of supervision to the training of youth workers, and that the time factor should be considered only in relation to a number of others. The question might arise as to whether many workers should be offered supervision for an inadequate period, or a few to a point where they no longer need it. The project can give no answer, but perhaps the content of this report indicates the possibilities of expansion and development in learning – for supervisors and workers – if training facilities are arranged.

THE YOUTH SERVICE IS NOT ALONE

While this report has been concerned with the supervision of youth workers, and with the development of their supervisory skill, the conclusions have already related this briefly to the supervision of students and part-time workers, and to other areas where supervisors might be found.

The purpose of the project was to learn within it and from it, and not to find out how much was happening in other spheres. But at the same time, no one imagined that this kind of exploration was unique, and that the youth service alone was interested in supervision. In social casework, where supervision originated, many more services are introducing supervision. The probation service, education, religious organisations, the marriage guidance council, and others have already introduced supervision, or are beginning to recognise its possibilities or importance in the training of workers. Why are we all working simultaneously in this way? Could it have anything to do with the need for the significance of the individual? Could it relate to the need to understand situations and people within them as opposed to applying rules? Could it relate to a recognition that people can be helped to learn for themselves instead of being taught?

These questions, and others, are affecting the interest in supervision simply because they reflect some of the needs and insights of society in general. In education, approaches to learning have been changing for some time – perhaps starting in primary schools, but now including adult education. In religion, many people are rejecting a dependence on an absolute, and are concerned with understanding, awareness, and an acceptance of change and its potential.

It must be significant, too, that whereas a few years ago the awakening interest in youth work was in understanding groups, there appears to have grown from this a concentration on the individual on the one hand and on communities on the other. Perhaps what is now required is indicated by the requirements of the supervision sessions; that each aspect – individual, group, community – might be explored separately, and then related to each other so that their relationship is understood in a new way.

Perhaps this same approach might be used in understanding the nature and potential of supervision. The thorough exploration of supervision in separate settings – case work, group work, community work, youth work, education – could be followed by a sharing of knowledge and experience, in which the common element and the differences are understood. This might lead to a network within a community, in which training is shared and supervisors are available and prepared to help workers in a variety of settings.

The Addition of Group Training

AN analysis of the project seminars, which numbered thirty-three, could provide material for a second full report. As the main interest in the project was supervision, this appendix is included to describe the group training only as it related to the individual training. Suggestions have been made in the youth service that group training might well take the place of individual training – that 'group supervision' could be developed. But this report emphasises the individual nature of supervision – that supervision is a recognition of the particular needs of a worker in a particular job, and of the learning which is possible in a two-person relationship. Group training meets other needs and achieves different purposes.

Regular meetings of participants in the project had a three-fold purpose. The first was to enable the workers to support each other. They had a common interest – learning to supervise – and through coming together were able to share experiences and problems. They were able to use the same language when describing these, and could expect to be understood, whereas in other settings they were constantly called upon to defend and explain what they were doing. Even though in the early days the value of this support was rarely discussed, the workers were aware, through their meetings, that they were not in isolation.

Secondly, through meeting as a group, workers were increasingly able to share in decisions for the ongoing programme of the project. At first they decided on the content of the group meetings, and on the part they wanted the tutor to play in the meetings. Later they decided on the arrangements for selecting supervisees. The number of group meetings in relation to supervision sessions then became a decision based on discussion of anyone's suggestion. Finally, everyone shared in the consideration of the extension of the project, of the meaning of supervision, and of the validity of the report, and also in explaining the project to people outside. In this way, the responsibility for the work in the project changed from being invested mainly in the tutor/supervisor, to being accepted by everyone concerned.

The third aspect of the purpose of group meetings, and the one of which everyone was aware at the beginning, was that learning within supervision should be supplemented by learning as a group. This meant that workers could learn from each other through sharing ideas, from testing out possibilities, from building up on suggestions and contributions and from the recognition of different approaches, different values, and different insights. It also gave an opportunity for theorising on practice, and for considering theories in relation to each other. Finally it enabled workers to understand their own participation and that of others, in a training group, and to relate this to learning about other groups.

The first agreed purpose of the group was therefore that participants should learn more about the work they were doing. The elements of support and increasing responsibility were secondary to the common task – that of understanding more about youth work (particularly work with groups), and later, about supervising. It was important that this purpose should be understood at the beginning, for although it was what the workers wanted, they, together with many other youth workers, were going through a period of self-consciousness and apprehension about participation in groups. Several thought that in any training group, the main subject for discussion would be their own behaviour.

An example of this expectation occurred at the beginning, when the tutor asked, giving alternatives, how they would like to consider the subjects agreed upon. One worker said it would be helpful if the tutor would open a discussion on the first subject. Several workers laughed self-consciously and one told the worker who had spoken that he was evading his responsibility, and asked his reason for making the suggestion. Someone then asked the tutor if she intended to explain to the group how it was behaving. The tutor reminded the group of its purpose, and this was discussed at some length. She then reminded the workers that they had been asked to make a choice, and one suggestion had been put forward for consideration. From this point onwards the emphasis in discussion was on subject matter, and the group's behaviour was considered only from time to time in relation to it.

The first training sessions indicated in several ways their value as a support to supervision. The main one was in the wealth of information available for discussion. Workers of different backgrounds, religions, values, knowledge and situations were able to share these with each other. Whereas in supervision, a worker was learning about himself in his own situation, in the group he was learning from several people

172

about a variety of situations. This was not only a useful experience in understanding material contributed by group members, but also in relating different knowledge and different aspects.

Sometimes a subject was chosen – for example, decision making in groups - and in discussion the numerous illustrations were provided by group members. This meant that conclusions were never easily reached – another aspect was frequently being presented for consideration. On occasions, when the subject was 'the structure of a centre', or 'volunteers', one worker's situation was used for discussion, and the rest of the group questioned him on it. At other times, records of incidents or groups were presented by one worker and explored by the group.

When using these and other methods, workers were not only using material from their own work, but were together finding different ways of exploring theories and situations, and of relating theory and practice. Also, through full participation they were extending the range of information with which to examine their work. It was inevitable that such discussions were not limited to experience within centres, but ranged through wider aspects of society – different professions and religions, governments, United Nations, trade unions, prisons, immigrants, communities and organisational structures.

The seminars also provided an opportunity for the study of professionalism. Confidentiality, non–judgementalism, self-determination or equality, were thrashed out in terms of particular people in particular situations. 'Confidentiality' was a question of whether one shared knowledge of Tom's problems with a volunteer, whether one should work only with Dick, or consult his parents too, or how far information could be shared with a particular probation officer. 'Equality' in supervision changed to a consideration of the particular contributions of a supervisor and a supervisee. 'Self-determination' was reflected on to individual needs, or the stages reached by different groups. No longer were such principles seen as a set of absolutes, but they were understood as words which raised innumerable questions, and suggested difficult choices when applied to people with whom one was working. Although similar examples arose in supervision, the group supplemented and speeded up the understanding of professional behaviour, and provided a setting in which new thinking could be tested with colleagues.

The group therefore broadened the area of learning. But as this was happening, supervision deepened it. In supervision, a worker was able to work through his particular problems, and understand his own situation and behaviour. It seemed increasingly evident, that for this reason the workers were able to concentrate on subjects and learn more fruitfully in the group. Individuals did not need to press for their problems and their difficulties to be discussed in the group – they were quickly able to distinguish between material appropriate for the group, and material appropriate for supervision. This meant that a worker was able to apply himself to the discussion of a subject even though it did not relate to his particular need at that time. It seemed therefore that supervision and group training could be complementary.

The group, being task-centred, reduced the strain on workers who in supervision were learning in a new way to understand their own work and their behaviour in it. But a task-centred group does not dispense with feelings. Also, when the task included a study of group behaviour, awareness of behaviour within the group became inevitable and useful. Feelings and awareness were present, and they were used, but they were secondary to the task.

Some workers commented at first in supervision on their inability to contribute in the group, or their concern that they were talking too much. These and other comments sometimes presented a dilemma to the supervisor who accepted such discussion as a part of supervision, but she also felt that if feelings were expressed to her, they were less likely to be expressed in the group. At that stage she was not sure of the effect of this on the group. If it were developed she might well be supporting ten individuals who should be supporting each other in the group. But the workers' concern lessened as they understood more clearly the task of the group, and how it related to supervision.

Each worker was aware in the group of his own relationship with the tutor/supervisor, and also that the other workers were being supervised. This affected spontaneity at times, and occasionally seemed to cause arguments which, without appearing on the surface to be so, were about the uncertainty which the workers were experiencing. Comments were made to the supervisor such as, 'You are the only one who knows about each of us'. It seemed important that these feelings should be accepted and understood insofar as they affected the task of the group. They were discussed when the group was evaluating or planning (which happened at intervals) and also, as mentioned earlier, in supervision.

For the first months, the workers were divided into two groups. At intervals, and without conscious effort, the groups began to use themselves as an illustration. When Group 2 discussed reasons for joining a group, workers gave their reasons for joining the project. When Group 1 felt they were not learning much from free discussion, they discussed what was happening in the group to prevent this. With these and other examples, workers began to relate their experience in the group to their learning about groups. Later different values in the group were noted. The roles accepted by group members were recognised – that one worker always opened the discussion, one tried to prevent argument, one always brought out a new aspect of a subject and prevented the group from moving on quickly. Later, it was noticed when workers changed roles, and sometimes one would experiment with a different role.

When the groups came together, it was to discuss supervision, and the change made very little impact. Only two workers had difficulty in adjusting to the larger group. Without preliminaries supervision was discussed and studied in four sessions. Then there was a break of four months during which most workers started to supervise. In this period the tutor was away for five weeks and there was no supervision. In the first session after the break, there was satisfaction at being together again and everyone brought each other up to date. But the subject being discussed was one about which each worker now had strong feelings. Not only was he in a new situation (supervising) which he found difficult, but he was also in competition with the others. He wanted to know bow he compared with the others and whether they had the same problems, but at first was unable to admit it. Therefore while the group was a support and feelings could be expressed in it, it was also a threat because no one could say what his problem – comparison – was. In the second session, the group seemed to fall apart. Each one commented on difficulties in supervising and frequently managed to pursue his own line of thought without listening to anyone else. No one was satisfied with the outcome. In the next session, one worker commented that he wished he knew how others were faring in comparison to himself. This in part reduced the tension, and specific problems were discussed by almost everyone. Two sessions later anxieties and worries about supervising and not being able to supervise were thrashed out and recognised in the group, and at the same time it was agreed that the training should be extended.

During this period, which started in the middle of the project and lasted from four to six sessions, the group appeared to have a particular part to play. While each worker was learning in his own supervision, how he supervised, he also needed very strongly to understand himself as a supervisor in relation to other supervisors. Although this had not been anticipated, the group provided the setting in which this need could be met, and some of the concern understood and resolved.

By the time the report was presented, chapter by chapter, and in its first draft, workers were ready to discuss it. They could see themselves in the content and note similarities and differences in experience. This led to a consideration of common elements and individual differences in supervision, and to comparisons of different situations. It was at this stage too that workers were more fully aware of their own group behaviour, and could discuss this in a more detached way, similar to their discussion of their work.

Group training in the project therefore seemed to have at least two valuable functions. It provided the setting in which workers could relate their own understanding and situation to a variety of others. It was therefore complementary to the more intensive study in supervision, and was more fruitful because of this study. The group also made it possible for workers to test out their attitudes and ideas, and express their feelings about a new situation – that of supervising – with their colleagues. This helped them, not only to learn more in supervision, but to become more objective about supervision when discussing it with colleagues inside and outside the group.

Bibliography

GROUP WORK SETTING

M. Williamson	*Supervision - new patterns and processes*	Association Press, N.Y. 1961
G. Wilson and G. Ryland	*Social Group Work Practice*	Houghton Mifflin 1949
	European Seminar on the General Principles of SG W	United Nations 1960
Council of Europe	*Training the full-time youth worker*	Council of Europe 1962
J. E. Matthews	*Working with Youth Groups*	University of London Press 1966

SOCIAL CASEWORK

J. S. Heywood	*An Introduction to Teaching Casework Skills*	Routledge and Kegan Paul 1964
F. Biestek	*The Casework Relationship*	Allen and Unwin 1961

EDUCATION

W. R. Niblett, ed.	*How and Why do we Learn ?*	Faber and Faber Ltd. 1965
C. M. Fleming	*The Social Psychology of Education*	Routledge and Kegan Paul 2nd ed. 1963

M. F. Cleugh	*Educating Older People*	Tavistock Publications 1962
M. L.J. Abercrombie	*Anatomy of Judgment*	Hutchinson 1960
C. Towle	*The Learner in Education for the Professions*	Cambridge University Press 1954

SUPERVISION – PUBLISHED ARTICLES

K. McDougall	Training social workers	*New Society,* 8.10.64
E. Younghusband	Social work training	*New Society,* 1.11.62
H. I. Evans	School practice and its problems	*Teacher in Wales,* No. 4, 15.5.64
E. R. Clarkson	Thoughts on the supervision of mature students	*Case Conference,* X 6, Nov. 1963
D. M. Deed	Dangers of stereotypes in student supervision	*Case Conference,* IX I, May 1962
N. Timms	A time-study of supervision	*Case Conference,* IX 3, July 1962
H. M. Zach	Supervision – a treatise in its defence	*Almoner,* XVII, 7, 1964
F. Berl	The content and method of supervisory teaching	*Social Casework,* XLIV, 9, 1963
H. A. Otto and K. A. Griffith	A new approach to developing the student's strength	*Social Casework,* XLIV 3, 1963
E. Stiles	Supervision in perspective	*Social Casework,* XLIV 1, 1963
R. B. Woodings	In-service training	*Accord,* VIII 3, 1963